Save Efficient Internet For Smart Transportation

Jay J. Moses

ABSTRACT

With the rise of smart vehicles, an intelligent transportation system (ITS) has been considered as becoming a reality. An ITS offers a huge potential to improve road safety, traffic congestion and even optimize fuel consumption to a great deal. However, when the vehicle density is high, the performance of Internet of Vehicles (IoV), which is regarded as network of smart vehicles, suffers due to the broadcast storm problem. To address this issue, this dissertation investigates a novel clustering approach to build stable clusters of vehicles using behavioral parameters and a current journey parameter. Using the parameters, the proposed approach calculates a Cluster Fitness Score (CFS) for each vehicle and a vehicle with the highest CFS in a cluster is selected as a Cluster Head (CH) for that cluster. The CH then is responsible to coordinate and manage all the communications originating from the cluster based on the changing traffic scenario. Furthermore, the approach also investigates contention window adaptation to reduce channel contention and thus improve IoV's network performance. The performance of the proposed approach demonstrates better cluster stability and improved network performance when compared with prior approaches.

The tremendous volume of data produced in the Internet of Vehicles (IoV) presents an opportunity to utilize machine learning (ML) for developing several intelligent services. The distributed vehicles equipped with varieties of smart sensors exchanging information with server(s) offer a significant potential to achieve intelligent transpiration system. This form of learning has demonstrated a proliferation and enhancement of varieties of IoT applications and services in recent times [1]. However, the abundance of data produced in IoV also gives rise to significant communication challenges when attempting to efficiently implement centralized learning (CL). To address this challenge, we propose a novel approach to utilize Mahalanobis distance (MD) metric for sampling the data produced by the IoV network. In the proposed approach, vehicles transmit their data to the nearby roadside infrastructure (RSI), which then samples valuable data from the available data using MD metric and relays it to the central server for necessary learning tasks. The sampling ratio for every RSI is determined to satisfy the estimated network delay required to transmit the data to the central server. The proposed method of transmitting only the valuable data, offers the huge potential to establish a communication-efficient learning network for the Internet of Vehicles. Initially, the learning performance of the proposed system is evaluated on synthetic data, followed by testing it on a real data to demonstrate its effectiveness.

While the centralized learning approach offers a significant advantage in terms of aggregating data and leveraging substantial computing resources to create high-quality Machine Learning (ML) models, it also presents privacy issues when sending data from vehicles to a server. This can potentially raise safety concerns in IoV. In recent times, ML is on the verge of transitioning from centralized, distributed to federated learning (FL) due to the inherent privacy-preserving framework provided by FL. FL enables collaborative learning from participants just by exchanging updated model parameters with the FL server while keeping training data local in the connected vehicles. However, this learning framework makes the life of the server difficult to detect the malicious behavior of participants. To this end, this dissertation investigates a novel approach to leverage Shiryaev's Quickest Change Detection (QCD) technique in the FL realm to detect anomaly in the model parameters sent by the connected vehicles. The peculiarities of the proposed approach are that it can detect anomaly in the individual client level and detect anomaly in the aggregated model. Furthermore, it does not add any computation overhead in the client side and communication overhead during transmission.

QCD approach is useful to detect anomaly in the exchanged information however, it can not prevent the man-in-the-middle type attacks and the possible trust and malfunctioning issues linked with a centralized server. To address these issues, this dissertation investigates blockchain (BC) empowered federated learning (FL) for IoV. To make the BC based system efficient, this study proposes a novel way to investigate information dissemination delay in BC based internet of vehicles (IoV) using small world network based peer selection strategy. Additionally, this study also incorporates IoV specific informed decision for peer selection to facilitate even faster dissemination of information in the network and make BC based system efficient. Network topology of vehicles is represented using a graph approach and based on that the information dissemination delay is formulated. The delay is compared between scenarios when peer selection strategy uses informed decision and that does not use informed decision. The performance of the proposed approach is evaluated through the graph analysis and which demonstrates that the inclusion of informed decision reduces the information dissemination delay remarkably.

TABLE OF CONTENTS

LIST OF TABLES

xiii

LIST OF FIGURES

xvi

LIST OF ABBREVIATIONS

xvii

A | B | C | D | F | H | I | M | Q | R | S | V

A

API Application Interface.

B

BC blockchain.

C

CFS Cluster Fitness Score.
CH Cluster Head.

D

DSRC Dedicated Short-Range Communications.

F

FL Federated Learning.

H

HE homomorphic encryption.

I

IoT Internet of Things.
IoV Internet of Vehicles.
ITS Intelligent Transportation System.

M

MD Mahalanobis Distance.
MITM Man-in-the-middle.
ML Machine Learning.

Q

QCD Quickest Change Detection.

R

RG Random Graph.
RL Regular Lattice.
RSI Road Side Infrastructure.

S

SMC secure multi-party computation.
SW Small World.

V

V2I Vehicle-to-Infrastructure.
V2V Vehicle-to-Vehicle.
VANET Vehicular-Ad-Hoc-Network.
VoI Value of Information.

CHAPTER 1.   INTRODUCTION

1.1   Internet of Vehicles Towards Intelligent Transportation System

Lately, the number of vehicles and the miles they are driven have increased at a faster pace [2]. Traffic congestion has been a big problem and is likely to climb further in the near future. In 2018 alone, 1.35 million people died due to road accidents [3]. So, an Intelligent Transportation System (ITS) has been a necessity to provide timely safety and other traffic information to the vehicles. With the rapid advancement in vehicular technologies, communication technologies, smart sensors, ML and others, it is believed that smart autonomous vehicles will solve the existing transportation problems. Major contributors to the transportation problems like congestion and accidents are human errors and ambiguity. IoV capable of sensing the environment and communicating with neighboring vehicles and infrastructures to exchange every bit of required information for safe navigation, detecting hurdles, optimizing routes and others on-the-fly, offers a true potential to realize ITS for effective traffic management and road safety [4]. IoV has been an active area of research to envision as a solution to achieve an intelligent transport system (ITS) for the past few decades.

In IoV, each vehicle is equipped with various smart sensors, dedicated short-range communication (DSRC) technology based on the IEEE 802.11p standard and cellular communication that enable sharing and exchanging of information wirelessly among vehicles using vehicle-to-vehicle (V2V) and vehicle-to-infrastructure (V2I) communications [2]. Vehicles are expected to exchange basic safety messages periodically as well as other information such as collision warning, lane change information, emergency warning, up-to-date traffic information, active navigation, infotainment, and so on. Cellular infrastructures and road side units (RSU) are placed beside the roads to provide road safety, navigation, infotainment, and other roadside services. A system model for IoV is shown in Figure 1.1.

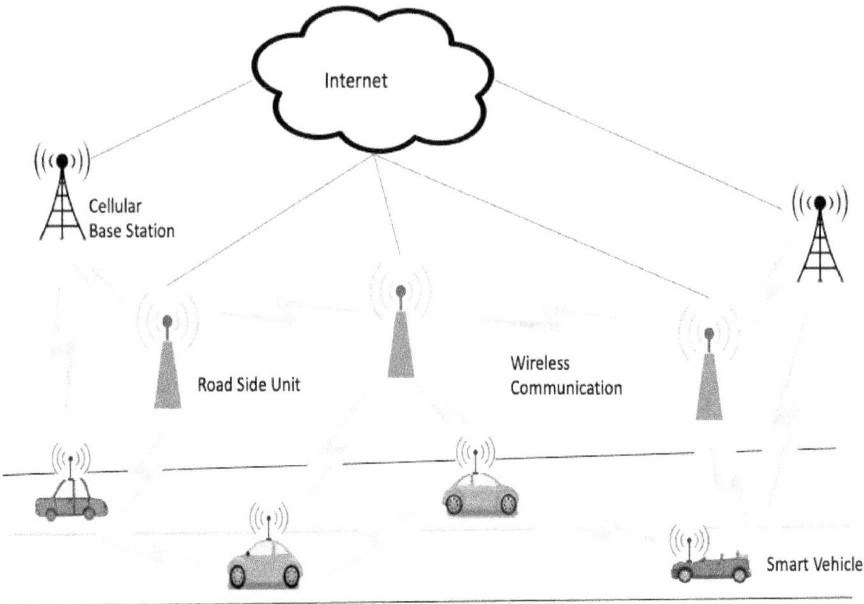

Figure 1.1. System Model for Internet of Vehicles

IoV aims to provide safety and other services however, its performance degrades when vehicular density is high. Clustering in IoV is well investigated approach to tackle such situation. Most of the clustering approaches however, do not well investigate stability of clusters which in fact is highly important considering the high mobility of vehicles. Instability of clusters results in high cluster management activities which could make IoV less efficient and may have adverse effect on the performance of IoV. To this end, this dissertation works towards designing clusters which not only have better stability but also improves the network performance of IoV. Furthermore, a contention window adaptation approach is also incorporated on top of clustering to enhance the performance of IOV further.

Smart vehicles heavily rely on the ML algorithm(s) running on them to determine their actions based on data collected from various smart sensors, neighboring vehicles, and infrastructure. ML has become an essential part of our daily lives, not only improving user experience and business modeling, but also discovering and preventing cyber threats. The large volume of data generated in the IOV is the most potential contributor to the success of Intelligent Transportation Systems (ITS). Service providers use use collaborative ML paradigm to produce the highly intelligent services where ML models are trained with aggregated data received from the connected devices.

This approach of learning termed as centralized learning, may pose communication concerns as the number of smart vehicles equipped with different types of IoT devices increases. Not all vehicles may have valuable information to contribute to enhance collaborative learning. Therefore, excluding such vehicles and selecting only those with useful observations presents an opportunity to create a communication-efficient learning environment. To achieve this goal, this dissertation explores a novel approach to sampling observations based on their Value of Information (VoI), which is measured using theMahalanobis Distance (MD) metric. The lower the distance, the higher the VoI is considered. The underlying assumption for using the MD metric is that sensor observations are normally distributed by nature [5]. Based on this assumption, valuable observations are selected and sent to the centralized server for necessary ML tasks. When an RSI receives observational data from sensors, it samples the data using the MD metric, and the sampling ratio is determined by the estimated network delay to reach the server. The performance of this sampling approach, which suits the available communication cost without noticeable performance loss, is compared to the standard approach that considers all data.

Although, the proposed centralized learning framework offers a huge potential to realize a communication-efficient learning framework for the IoV, it may pose serious security and privacy threats in IoV. An exponential rise of heterogeneous smart vehicle sensors and furthermore, communicating over a wireless medium, has extended the attack surface significantly. Wireless communication networks' standards and protocols are more vulnerable than wired communication networks. The mobile and distributed nature of the smart devices exaggerates the security challenges even more. The consequences of cyber-attacks are relatively more serious in the IoV environments compared to other domains as it has a direct impact on human life. It is possible that a maliciously controlled vehicle may cause disastrous consequences in roadways.

Considering all the highlighted issues above, an emerging framework of learning introduced by Google [6] which is termed as Federated Learning (FL) better fits with IoV network. In FL, ML tasks are performed in the end devices and instead of sending data to the server, only learning model parameters are sent. Server then aggregates parameters received from such devices and send the global parameters back to the devices. Connected devices then update the learning model with the global parameters. This privacy preserving framework also enhances security by making the life of an attacker difficult to infer from the model parameters. Furthermore, as only model parameters are exchanged between end devices and server, it reduces the communication latency. However, with so much of promising offerings, some novel types of attacks named as poisoning and reverse engineering (e.g. [7], [8]) have been pointed in FL recently. In this regard, this dissertation investigates a novel approach to leverage QCD in server side to detect to detect anomaly in the exchanged model parameters. QCD is used to analyze the statistical properties of the model parameters and detect anomalous vehicles to make FL for IoV secure. Once malicious clients are identified, they can be excluded from the FL activities. Compared to other existing approaches, the proposed approach does not incur any computation burden to clients and furthermore, no extra communication cost is required. Applying QCD may not be able to detect malicious clients if they client act malicious from the beginning. To tackle this scenario, QCD is applied on the global model to identify anomaly caused by the model parameters sent by such malicious clients. Once detected, a service provider may discard the current global version and roll back to a past version.

In FL setting, although only ML parameters are exchanged between the clients and a server, it may still be vulnerable to different types of attacks. An attacker may perform Man-in-the-middle (MITM) attacks to forge the model update in transit or just to overhear communication to reveal the privacy of a user. A genuine client may be flagged by QCD and excluded from FL network because of an attacker in middle. Last but not least, the presence of a centralized server can also bring single point of failure and trust issues in FL. A server may favor some clients and skew the global model accordingly [9]. A client remains fully unaware about the fairness of the global model. To this end, it looks obvious to realize that, a trust-less network system is essential for collaborative learning in IoV. Taking all these issues into account, the dissertation also investigates leveraging BC in the FL for IoV. BC is a decentralized distributed network that uses public key cryptography, distributed digital ledger and consensus algorithms as core components for creating secure, transparent and audit-able network to allow people/devices to communicate in a trust-less manner (without presence of any intermediaries). However, using BC in FL incurs overheads that may affect the performance of FL for delay sensitive IoV operations. BC management activities add high computational and communication cost to the network. Assuming smart vehicles are equipped with high computing resources, this dissertation only investigates communication concern associated with BC. In a BC, each information/transaction created in any network node needs to be disseminated through out the network. A faster dissemination of information in the network reduces the communication cost of a BC network. The information dissemination process encapsulates peer based information dissemination strategy. In this respect, this dissertation finally investigates information dissemination delay and presents Small World (SW) network based peer selection approach to spread the information faster.

Lastly, IoV offers a huge potential to realize a true ITS with the ability to reduce traffic accidents and traffic congestion by a great deal while making the travel comfort and smoother. This dissertation explores the security and performance aspects of IoV and works toward creating an efficient, secure and trustworthy ITS.

1.2 Performance and Security Basics for Internet of Vehicles

Road safety and traffic congestion have been major problems and will continue to rise in the future as the number of vehicles in the road is increasing rapidly. So, an ITS expected to provide upcoming traffic information, detecting hurdles, optimizing routes and others promptly, has been essential for effective traffic management and road safety. Significant efforts have been dedicated by the government, companies, and academia worldwide for the research, development, and testing of ITS. For ITS, IoV is the backbone for sharing and exchanging information to support a wide range of road safety and infotainment applications.

In IoV, vehicles are expected to exchange safety and other messages timely. To achieve this, each vehicle is equipped with technologies that allow sharing and exchanging of information wirelessly between vehicles and infrastructures using Vehicle-to-Vehicle (V2V) and Vehicle-to-

Infrastructure (V2I) communications. Between these two forms of communication, V2V is the most prominent to realize IoV. Regular V2I communication is not guaranteed as it needs the presence of infrastructure throughout the roadside which requires a huge amount of investment. In IoV, each vehicle is equipped with dedicated short-range communication (DSRC) technology based on the IEEE 802.11p standard [10]. IEEE 802.11p inherits Enhanced Distributed Channel Access (EDCA) from 802.11e to provide a different level of quality of service (QoS) in ITS. To achieve this, it prioritizes different types of frames by assigning it to different access categories (AC) as shown in Table 2.3.

IEEE 802.11p standard is based on carrier sense multiple access/collision avoidance (CS-MA/CA) and supports DSRC communication between V2V/V2I for short-range up to 1 km. In IoV, each vehicle broadcasts its BSM every 100 milliseconds (ms) for the safety purpose. So, when the vehicle density increases, 802.11p suffers from channel congestion and packet collision. This restricts vehicles to broadcast its message prompting a high risk to vehicle safety [11]. In IoV, vehicles operate in highly dynamic environments on account of the presence of hidden stations, high mobility, channel fading (due to the stationary and mobile obstructions and other interference sources), and limited spectral bandwidth. Due to the delay constraint, the vehicles communicate based on 802.11 DCF without any request to send (RTS), clear to send (CTS), and acknowledgment signals [10]. The rate of network congestion, packets drop, and packet collision increases with the increase in vehicle density.

Smart sensors in vehicles such as global positioning system (GPS), radio detection and ranging (RADAR), light detection and ranging (LiDAR), cameras, etc. are expected to capture a tremendous volume of data. The enormous volume of data has contributed to develop a data-driven machine learning (ML) and deep learning (DL) models and create and improve varieties of services [12]. The mobile and distributed nature of the smart devices in IoV attracts different security challenges. The consequences of cyber-attacks are relatively more serious in the IoV environment compared to other domains as it has a direct impact on drivers' or passengers' life. A maliciously controlled vehicle traveling at 60 to 70 miles/hour on the highway can lead to a disastrous accident resulting in several deaths and injuries. To realize an efficient and effective ITS, a system of learning, which not only provides road safety and other traffic-related services but also be able to identify any kind of anomalies and intrusion and take corrective measures, must be in place. Traditional methods of countering cybersecurity issues protect devices only after the occurrence of specific types of attacks. However, the types and patterns of attacks in today's cyberspace have changed drastically. Attacks using polymorphic viruses keep changing their signatures and are difficult to identify and foretell. So, the ML approach of detecting and predicting threats, anomalies, or any kind of security breach in cyberspace and taking corresponding countermeasures is gaining so much attention in recent years. To cope with the rise in possible privacy and security threats, ML paradigm has transitioned from centralized, distributed to federated learning. Federated learning facilitates collaborative learning only by exchanging updated model parameters (between end devices and server) while data remains on end devices and the training is performed locally [6]. Theoretically, FL provides a very good privacy-preserving learning framework and which makes it highly suitable to be applied in IoV application. Beyond standard IoV services, a service provider may use FL to create and improve varieties of services and security solutions not only to provide better user experience but also to make IoV environment more secure and efficient.

1.3 Related Methods and Technologies

As highlighted in the previous sections, this dissertation investigates the performance and security aspects of IoV towards creating ITS. This section presents introduction to the main underlying methods and technologies considered for the proposed works.

1.3.1 Clustering

Clustering is a task of grouping a set of objects into multiple groups in such a way that objects in the same group are more similar (in some sense) to each other than to those in other groups [13]. Clustering has been applied to many fields for data analysis, pattern recognition, image analysis and others. In IoV research, clustering has been investigated particularly to improve its network performance. Clusters in IoV network are formed by associating mobile nodes (vehicles) into multiple groups as per the defined rule and within a group, mostly, a vehicle is selected as a CH. Primary role of a CH is to mediate between inside and outside of the cluster in a similar sense as a wireless access point [14]. An example of clustering of vehicles is shown in Fig. 1.2.

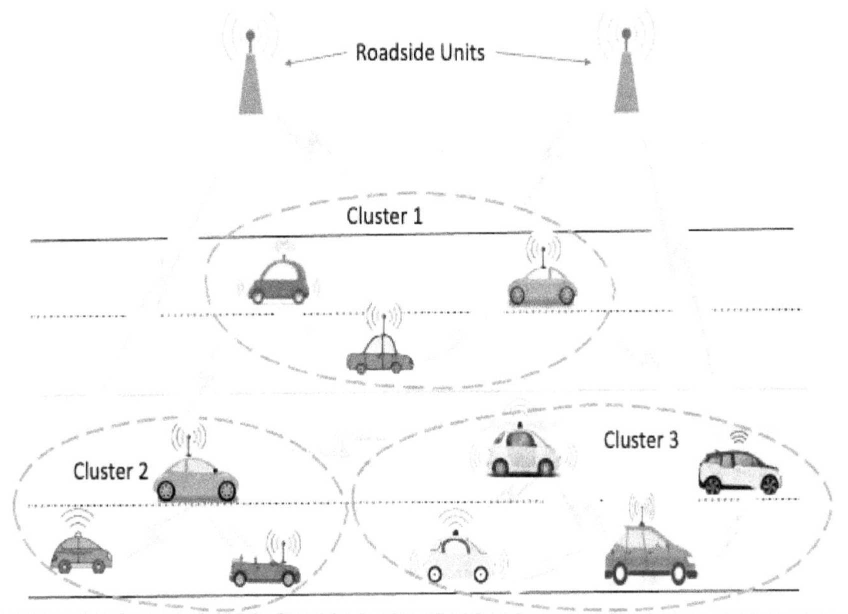

Figure 1.2. Clusters of Vehicles

Clustering works in IoV are differ to each other mainly on the approach of selecting CH and assigning it with the responsibilities. In most approaches, CH is selected based on a some kind of fitness score calculated from different parameters or metrics. Varieties of parameters such as distance, relative velocity, acceleration, turning direction, driver intention, trust level, propagation delay ratio, and others have been considered to calculate a fitness score. Majority of clustering works preferred to maintain single a CH while others took approach to maintain two CHs or some form of backup CH for efficient cluster management.

Despite the different approaches followed, clusters in IoV are expected to be robust against nodes' mobility, dynamic channel condition and cluster topology, and should guarantee efficient and reliable communication in IoV network.

1.3.2 Quickest Change Detection

QCD is a sequential analysis technique to detect change in the statistical properties of a stochastic system. In this technique, the stochastic process is continuously monitored through the sequential time series observations and when the observations undergo a change in the distribution due to a change or anomaly, an observer needs to raise an alarm as quickly as possible subject to minimum false alarm. Once the change is declared, a mitigating strategies are taken [15]. QCD techniques have been utilized in broad range of fields ranging from science, engineering, business and others. Among several applications, QCD techniques have also been successfully applied to detect intrusion and anomaly in the network systems.

Since the first proposal [16], QCD problems have been explored in both Bayesian as well as non-Bayesian settings. Shiryaev studied QCD problem in Bayesian setting and formulate optimal solution to minimize expected detection delay (EDD) subject to Probability of False Alarm (PFA) constraint for i.i.d. model [17, 18]. Other variations of QCD for the non-Bayesian setting and/or non-i.i.d model are only asymptotically optimal.

To illustrate QCD to detect a change in the mean of a Gaussian random sequence, Figure 1.3a depicts the path of the samples of a stochastic sequence which are distributed with mean 0 and variance 1 before the change, and after the change, the samples are distributed as mean 0 and variance 1. In the plot, it is hard to detect a change through by manual inspection. Where as, Figure. 1.3b shows the evolution of Shiryaev's statistic for the samples of Figure. 1.3a and as shown in figure, it stays close to 0 before the change point, and climbs abruptly to cross a threshold after the change point.

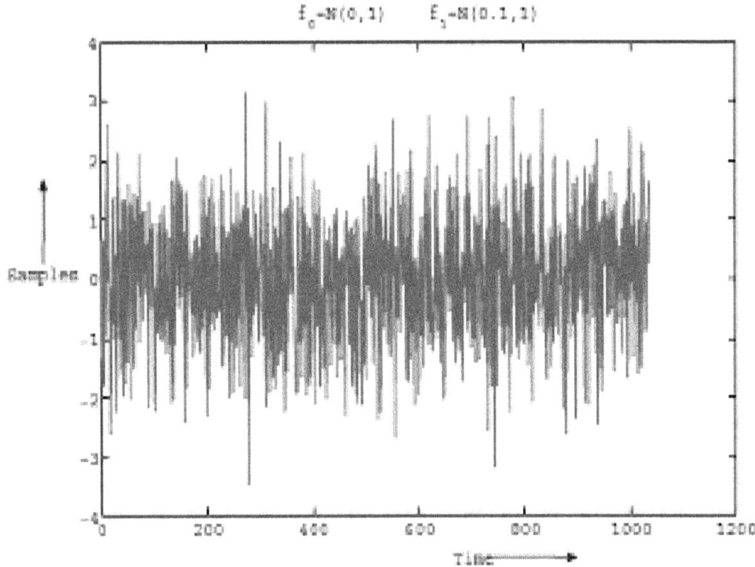

(a) Stochastic sequence with samples $f_0 \in N(0,1)$ before the change (time slot 500), and with samples from $f_1 \in N(0.1,1)$ after the change [15].

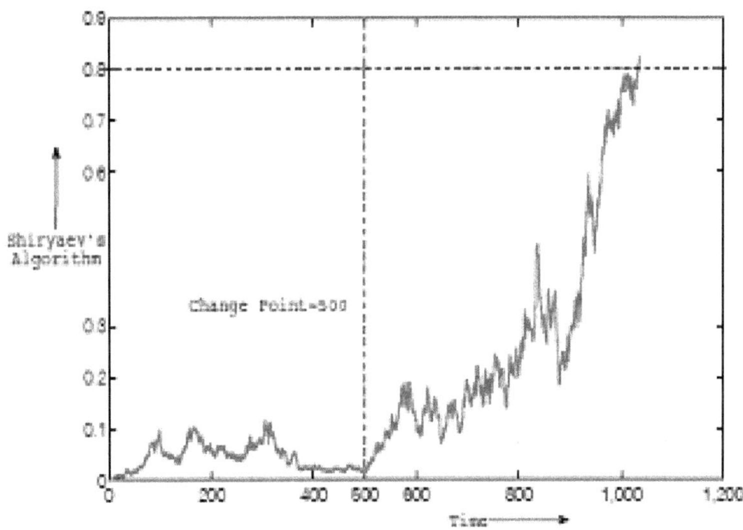

(b) Evolution of the classical Shiryaev algorithm when applied to the samples on the Figure. 1.3a. Change is detected approximately at time slot 1000 [15].

Figure 1.3. Detecting a change in the mean of distribution.

In this study, Shiryaev's formulations are leveraged and adapted to the FL scenario to detect malicious vehicles based on the statistical properties of model updates send by vehicles.

1.3.3   Centralized Learning Model

This model uses cloud-centric architecture (e.g.[19–22]) where data sent from end devices is centrally stored and processed in the cloud. In the cloud, data is analyzed, features are extracted and then models are built on top of the stored data. Models are accessed by the end devices sending requests through an Application Interface (API). This approach offers significant advantages but carries some serious issues. One big advantage of this approach is that the cloud offers a huge repository so that storing huge volumes of data sent by all the clients will not be problematic. Another advantage is that the cloud is mostly equipped with high-performance servers. These benefits facilitate the building of better-trained models. Moreover, cloud services are best protected by service providers for any security breaches or attacks. Offering such great advantages, this approach has serious concerns over privacy, security, and latency. All the data needs to travel to the cloud through insecure communication links makes the data vulnerable to being hacked by adversaries. All the private data generated by the devices are stored in the cloud raises big privacy concerns. Further, the central authority or the cloud service provider has all the control over the model and data. Additionally, as data needs to travel to and from the cloud, latency and bandwidth costs could be big issues if the communication distance between device and cloud is high. The working model of centralized learning is shown in Fig. 1.4.

1.3.4   Federated Learning

FL is a collaborative learning model where a general or pretrained model is distributed to network clients initially. With the local data, all the clients personalize their model by performing ML tasks locally and send its updated parameters to the FL server. The server then aggregates all the updates received from the clients and perform ML tasks and finally distributes the updated model to the clients [23]. The process of updating global model is iterative.

The working model of FL is shown in Fig. 1.5. This learning model first formulated by [6] is

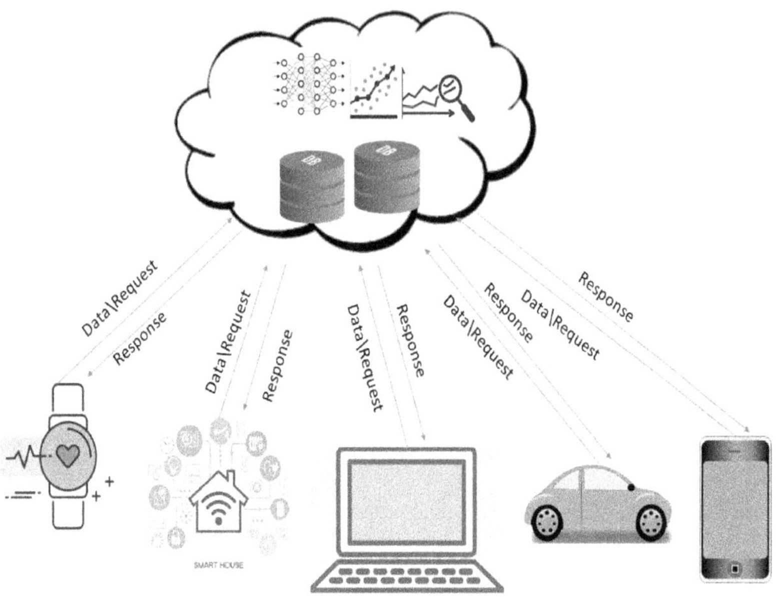

Figure 1.4. Centralized learning model for Internet of Things

as follows:

$$f(w) = \sum_{k=1}^{K} \frac{n_k}{n} F_k(w) \text{ Where } F_k(w) = \frac{1}{n_k} \sum_{i \in P_k} f_i(w) \tag{1.1}$$

In equation 1.1, $f_i(w)$ represents a loss function of prediction for input x_i to an expected output y_i with weight vectors w. K is the number of participants in current learning round and $F_k(w)$ is the local objective function of k_{th} participant. For total number of samples n, n_k is the number of samples present locally in k_{th} participant. Similarly, P_k with $n_k = |P_k|$, is the partitioned assigned to k_{th} participant from whole dataset P.

In a typical FL setting, when a device downloads the current model parameters (weight) from the server first, it initializes the local model with the downloaded parameters and then the local dataset is used to train the model. The parameters are optimized by minimizing local objective function that uses stochastic gradient descent (SGD). The optimized parameters from all such devices are sent to the server where they are aggregated using FederatedAveraging algorithm [6].

This way the global model is updated and the learning takes place.

As raw data resides locally on the device and only ML parameters are sent to the server, FL ensures privacy of the raw data of clients and complies with privacy policies and/or regulations e.g. The European Data Protection Regulation "General Data Protection Regulation (GDPR)" [24].

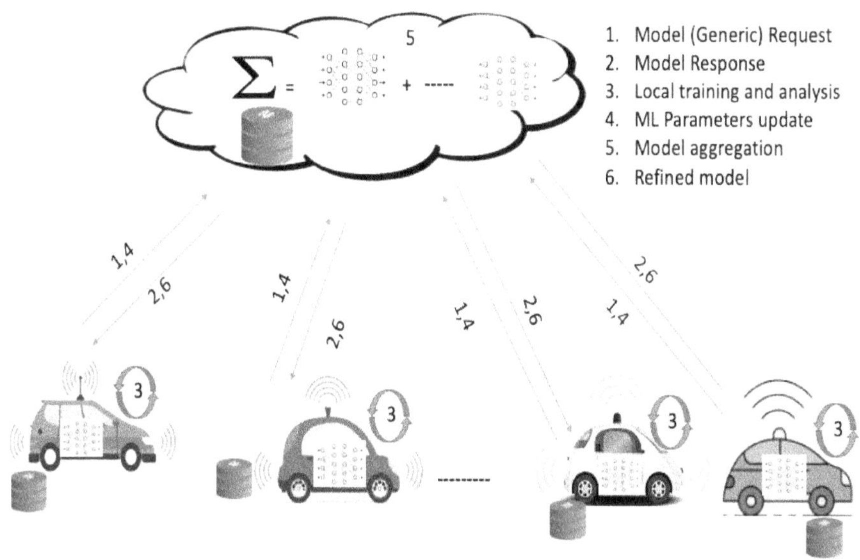

Figure 1.5. Federated learning model for Internet of Vehicles

The learning framework of FL is not only helpful to preserve the privacy of vehicles, but also strengthens security and improves communication latency. Considering these promising potentials, this dissertation works toward using to FL to create an ITS.

1.3.5 Blockchain

Although the concept of Blockchain has been in existence since 2008, it has been in the limelight just recently, thanks to the widespread success of cryptocurrency platforms (blockchain applications) like Bitcoin [25] and Etherium [26]. BC is a technology that allows people/devices to communicate in a secure and trustless manner without any intermediaries. It is a distributed network that records every exchanged information between parties in an immutable distributed database called a digital ledger. Figure 1.6 shows an example of blockchain network and its fundamental components.

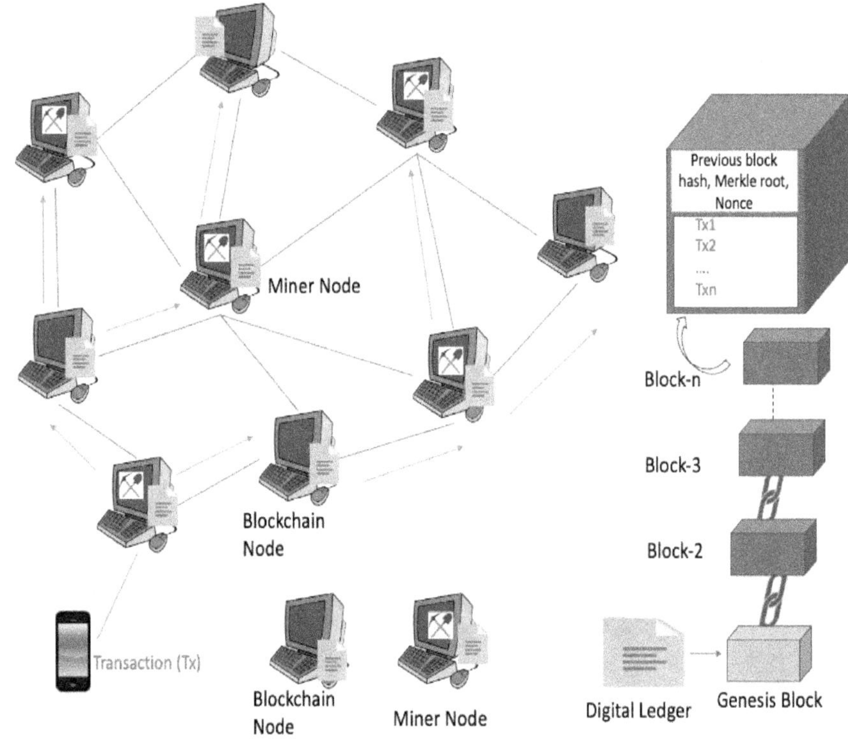

Figure 1.6. An example of a Blockchain Network

BC uses public key cryptography, distributed ledger, and consensus algorithms as core components to offer unparalleled benefits of security, transparency, and traceability (to any transactions that ever happened). It uses probabilistic proof of work (PoW) algorithm based consensus to create a block containing data in the form of transactions [25]. The blocks are stored chronologically creating a chain between blocks. The chain is maintained by cryptographic principles. Each block holds multiple records of transactions that occurred within some time period and a block header that contains two important information which are the previous block address and Merkle root [25]. Merkle tree root is a kind of fingerprint of all the information on the BC that is useful to validate the consistency of all the information of the BC. It changes even if any tiny bit of information on the BC changes. Merkle root is basically a binary tree root created from combining hashes of all the transactions. It is used to validate any transaction that occurred at any time.

A cryptographic hash function is applied to each block to make it immutable. Creating a current block, the hash function also takes into account the hash of the previous block to maintain a chain of blocks. Every created block is distributed and managed in the form of a digital ledger by a cluster of computers (nodes) connected to the BC network. This ledger contains a time-stamped series of all the records of data. It is immutable because any change in a ledger must be verified by the consensus of all the nodes. It is decentralized, secure, and transparent. This network does not belong to any central authority. The same digital ledger is shared with all and so, almost impossible to forge the entire network. Furthermore, everyone can see all the information along with its history. In a BC, when a transaction is initiated, it is distributed to the network. BC software running in each node of the network validates the transaction. Such transactions of some time period are collected separately in a block by powerful computers in the network acting as miners. These miners are rich in efficient computational resources consisting of Graphical Processing Unit (GPUs) or application-specific integrated circuit chips (ASICs) for intensive processing. These miners utilize their computational power for mining tasks. Which in fact is to solve a cryptographic mathematical puzzle to find a particular patterned cryptographic block header for the current block. Such utilization of computational resources to solve the cryptographic puzzle is termed as proof-of-work [25]. Whoever finds the correct hash for the in-hand block header first, gets the mining reward in the form of cryptocurrency. This newly created block has a unique address and holds a pointer or chain to the previous block. This chain is created to maintain the chronological history of all the blocks starting from the first block, which is also called genesis block. This is performed to achieve the integrity of transactions in BC. The new block is then distributed in the BC network and every participant adds this block to its respective ledger.

Theoretically blockchain guarantees security with the exception of 51% attack [27] however, it is considered as only hypothetical for any large network or network with high computing power. With all the promising potentials BC can offer, this dissertation investigates incorporating BC to

IoV to make IoV trustless, fully secure and transparent.

1.4   Problem Description

With the advancement of Information and Communication Technologies (ICT) and smart vehicles, ITS is envisioned as a solution to improve quality, effectiveness, and safety of future transportation system [28]. V2V using Dedicated Short-Range Communications (DSRC) is considered as the prominent form of communication in ITS to support a large class of road safety and traffic efficiency applications (e.g., collision avoidance, passing assistance, electronic-toll-collection, smart parking, and platooning) [28]. However, the V2V communication which is based on 802.11p, could be heavily affected due to high traffic and high mobility and can pose a risk to road safety. Clustering approaches have been mostly explored to address these issues and improve the IoV' network performance. Nevertheless, most of the existing approaches focused to improve the network performance without investigating the stability of clusters enough. Instability of clusters requires high cluster management activities which may in fact result in poor network performance. Contention window adaptation approach has also been sought as a solution to address IoV performance issues. However, combining these approaches could have the greater potentials to resolve the issues and which is still need to be explored.

The rapid growth in size and complexity of ML models and the exponential surge of Internet of Things (IoT) sensors is likely to bring communication concern over the efficient implementation of centralized learning. In IoV, the VoI of sensors' data could differ from vehicle to vehicle due to the different operating environments, equipped resources and others. An approach to sample vehicles based on the VoI to exclude those with the lower value of information from taking part in collaborative learning offers a huge potential to create a communication efficient learning environment.

Rapid development on IoT sensors has enabled the automotive industry to bring several applications to vehicles. Smart vehicles are equipped with cellular communication, bluetooth communication, regular radio communication and others to provide remote connectivity. This remarkable advantages however, have put a vehicle at risk to be easily hacked. To demonstrate the vulnerability, Miller and Valasek were able exploit car's cellular connectivity by taking 2014 Jeep Cherokee in control remotely to shut off the engine and disabling the brakes while a person driving a car [29]. In recent times, ML has been inevitable for service providers to deal with dramatic volume of data generated by vehicles and provide quality services to users. To produce quality models, in most common setting, service providers collect data from the vehicles centrally to aggregate the data and apply in the ML models. This learning approach put vehicles at greater privacy and security risks and associates high communication cost too. IOV operations usually utilize information which are highly time sensitive. With these considerations, IoV necessitates a secure and privacy preserving collaborative ML approach which is efficient to deliver all the information timely. FL, a recent introduction to privacy preserving collaborative ML framework, offers a huge potentials to enhance security and communication for IoV. In FL however, as only ML parameters are exchanged between the end devices and the server, it is quite difficult to detect malicious or compromised vehicles. For the safety of IoV environment, an efficient approach is required to analyze the exchanged model parameters and detect such vehicles.

The distributed vast varieties sensors and wireless communication standards and protocols used in IoV have made IoV network vulnerable to MITM types attacks also. An attacker in the middle could easily lunch poisoning and reverse engineering attacks that are specific to FL. Such attacks pose a security and safety threats to individual vehicle and IoV network and it needs to be addressed.

BC is a disruptive technology to create a trustless, immutable and traceable network and has made its way to numerous usecases [30]. BC has the potential to create fully secure and trustless ITS. However, BC could be inefficient to meet the time constraint of IoV services due to the overhead of BC management activities. An efficient and effective approach towards making BC applicable to IoV needs to be well explored.

1.5 Objectives

The objectives of this dissertation are as follows:

1. To design, develop and evaluate the stable clusters to improve the network performance of the IoV.

2. To design, develop and evaluate a communication efficient machine learning framework for the IoV.

3. To design, develop and evaluate a mechanism to detect malicious clients in federated learning for the IoV.

4. To design, develop and evaluate a fully secure and efficient blockchain empowered federated learning for the IoV.

1.6 Organization

This dissertation document is divided into 6 chapters. The introductory chapter (Chapter 1) highlights the motivations behind the proposed research, its background, the research problem descriptions, and its objectives. The following chapters present the works towards achieving a secure and efficient ITS. Specifically, Chapter 2 presents work aimed at improving the network performance of IoV. In this chapter, a novel clustering approach is presented, which builds stable clusters taking the behavioral and current journey parameters of vehicles into account. The work demonstrates how stable clusters can contribute to addressing the broadcast storm problem that is likely to arise due to high vehicular density. The proposed work also incorporates a novel contention window adaptation approach to enhance the network performance of IoV. This chapter also discusses different ways to reduce cluster management activities towards making the system efficient. Chapter 2 intends to fulfill objective 1 of the dissertation, and the realization of this research has been published in [31].

Chapter 3 presents the design, development, and evaluation of a sensor data selection approach based on the VoI. The approach aims to address communication concerns in centralized learning caused by the proliferation of smart vehicles. The proposed approach uses the MD metric to assess the VoI of sensor data. The evaluation demonstrates that selecting data with higher VoI achieves almost the same performance as considering all the data. Chapter 3 aims to meet objective 2 of the dissertation. The outcome of this study has been submitted to a conference and is currently under review.

Chapter 4 primarily focuses on securing IoV and presents the application of the QCD technique to detect anomalous vehicles. The work demonstrates how a server can analyze the model updates sent by the vehicles not only to detect anomalous vehicles but also to identify anomalous global model. Eliminating anomalous participants helps to enhance the accuracy of the global model and keep the learning environment safe. Chapter 4 is aimed at achieving objectives 3, and the realization of this research has been published in [32].

Chapter 5 presents a proposed work aiming to create fully secure ITS. This chapter considers the possible ways of attacks that were not considered in Chapter 4. This chapter specifically considers MITM attacks and trust and malfunctioning issues associated with a centralized server. It primarily investigates leveraging BC to create a fully secure FL environment for IoV. Although BC aims to provide a fully secure network, it incurs delay due to added overhead of BC management activities. Considering this, the proposed work also investigates an approach to make the BC-based IoV system efficient. This chapter primarily focuses to meet objectives 4 of this dissertation. The realization of this research is submitted to a journal and is currently under review.

Finally, Chapter 6 concludes this dissertation document.

CHAPTER 2. CLUSTERING FOR IMPROVING NETWORK PERFORMANCE OF INTERNET OF VEHICLES

2.1 Introduction

IoV plays an indispensable role in intelligent transportation system (ITS). Vehicles in IoV are required to broadcast its safety messages periodically in a certain geographical area for safety purpose. When the vehicle density is high, the blind broadcasting mechanism in IoV may cause high contention, collision and transmission among neighboring nodes likely to cause the broadcast problem. These situation could degrade the performance of IoV significantly to put vehicles at risk.

To address this issue, this chapter investigates a novel approach of clustering using a score calculated from trust value based on exchanged information, the total mileage of the vehicle, total mileage traveled with clusters, total disconnection count from clusters, and distance to travel in the current direction. Each vehicle posses a score based on these parameters named as cluster fitness score (CFS). A vehicle with the highest CFS acts as a CH for a cluster and coordinates communication among CMs. The CH then supervises two modes of communications which are CFC and CBC. In CFC, each CM is allowed to broadcast its BSM periodically without contention whereas in CBC, CMs are required to contend with RSUs, CHs, and other vehicles (non-cluster members) to broadcast its non-BSM messages. However, in CBC, we prioritize CH and external communicating parties to grab the communication channel early. The strategy here is to allow each CH to exchange information with external parties and disseminate any important information in and out of the cluster with lower network congestion. We do so by increasing contention window size (CW) of CMs and which is increased based on the speed, position and CFS of each CM. The roles of speed, position and CFS are explained in subsection 2.5.2. To improve the performance, CH arranges different number of CFC and CBC slots as per the number of CMs and average speed of a cluster. Furthermore, whenever a CM broadcasts its frame, its transmission range is determined according to the distance of CMs at an extreme positions of the cluster. This is necessary to reduce interference with nearby cluster. In our clustering approach, we have designed a cluster table based on the direction to follow after the upcoming intersection to allow efficient partitioning into sub-clusters and merging of sub-clusters. We discuss all these and cluster management in section 2.3. We have also incorporated a reward scheme to encourage CMs to be associated with a cluster.

Our main contributions include a novel approach of clustering that also incorporates reward scheme to strengthen building stable clusters and dynamic allocation of CFC and CBC slots to enable efficient communication while reducing channel congestion and collision. Specifically, our contributions include:

1. Developing a clustering approach that utilizes past behaviors, trust (based on exchanged information), and current journey of vehicles.

2. Incorporating CH supervised communications (CFC and CBC) for each cluster to reduce network congestion and packet collision in IoV.

3. Contention window adaptation of each CM based on its speed, position and CFS to improve the performance of IoV.

The main motivation of our work is to enhance IoV's network performance by building stable clusters. The reason behind considering behavioral metrics, current journey metric and reward scheme is to form stable clusters where the detachment of CMs and CHs from clusters occurs infrequently. The reward scheme rewards vehicles for being associated with a cluster and punish them for leaving cluster opportunistically. The incorporation of CH supervised CFC and CBC modes of communications, transmission range based on the geographical position of CMs, and the contention window adaption are to reduce channel congestion and packet collision in high vehicle density scenario.

The rest of the chapter is organized as follows. Section 2.2 discusses related works. Section 2.3 presents system model and proposed CFS based clustering. Cluster formation process and its management are discussed in Section 2.4. CH supervised communications and contention window adaption are presented in Section 2.5. Reward model is included in Section 2.6. Section 2.7 presents simulation results and performance evaluations. Finally, section 5.6 concludes the chapter.

2.2 Related Work

In IoV, vehicles operate in highly dynamic environments on account of the presence of hidden stations, high mobility, channel fading (due to the stationary and mobile obstructions and other interference sources), and limited spectral bandwidth. Due to the delay constraint, the vehicles communicate based on 802.11 DCF without any request to send (RTS), clear to send (CTS), and acknowledgment signals [10]. The rate of network congestion, packets drop, and packet collision increases with the increase in vehicle density. The deployment of sufficient infrastructure on the roadside to regulate communication is not feasible due to the need for a significant cost. To overcome these problems, most of the research works in IoV have been directed towards proposing various clustering approaches. Despite the diversity of clustering algorithms, most of the approaches share the same general procedure like electing a CH or CHs, scheduling the communication, aggregating data, management of cluster when a vehicle joins or leaves a cluster (e.g., [33–36]). The most fundamental differences among various approaches in clustering are found in way of electing a CH and its leadership role. For electing a CH, most of the works are based on calculating a score that quantifies the fitness to act as a cluster head. Varieties of metrics have been used to calculate a weighted fitness index. According to the survey [14] on 28 clustering approaches, authors considered metrics like distance, relative velocity, acceleration, turning direction, driver intention, trust level, propagation delay ratio, number of following cars, signal to noise ratio and packet forwarding ratio to calculate weighted cluster fitness index. In Position-based Prioritized Clustering (PPC) [37], authors used travel time and average relative velocity as metrics to calculate the index. Vehicular Weighted Clustering Algorithm (VWCA) [38] calculated the CH selection weighted score from vehicle direction, degree of connectivity, an entropy value calculated from the mobility of nodes in the network, and a distrust level based on the reliability of a node's packet relaying. In

[39], authors proposed Trust-dependent Ant Colony Routing (TACR) which combines position and velocity with Certificate Authority trust metrics to compute a weighted cluster head selection metric. User-Oriented Fuzzy-logic-based Clustering (UOFC) [40] considered vehicular velocity, position, and driver intention metrics to calculate a score using a fuzzy classifier. In [36], authors combined vehicle state, speed, position, set of cars within communication range, flow direction, and vehicle behavior to mark whether the vehicle takes an exit on the next side exit or not metrics to calculate CH selection index. Liu et al. worked toward enhancing stability of clusters by considering average lifetime of all clusters as an optimization goal [41].

Most of the works proposed in IoV clustering considered electing a single CH (e.g., [42], [43], [44]) while others opted for multiple CHs. In [33], authors proposed to elect two functional CHs in each cluster to avoid re-clustering in case a CH leaves the cluster. With similar motivation, some works (e.g., AMACAD [45], FLBA [46], and SCalE[36]) suggested maintaining a backup CH to tackle re-clustering in case of losing a CH.

Although varieties of clustering algorithms with different metrics have been proposed, our work is novel and unique as we have considered trust-based metric together with several other behavioral metrics and a metric from the current journey. Further, the inclusion of a reward scheme based on behavioral metrics encourages vehicles to be associated with a cluster.

Contention window size (CW) of media access control sublayer (MAC) plays a significant role to control transmission delay and collision in IoV. Smaller CW reduces transmission delay whereas it increases the frame collision in contention-based IEEE 802.11p [47]. To address this issue, CW adaptation has been proposed in several works by considering different parameters. Artimy et al.[48] considered vehicle density to adjust CW. In [49], an intelligent adaptive controller based on traffic density was devised to change CW. Adler et al. [50] performed CW adaptation based on the relevance of the message. Rawat et al. [51] considered locale vehicle density estimation and the instantaneous collision rate to change the CW size. Work presented in [52] took into account 1-hop neighbor density and number of vehicles heard during a time period as parameters to adapt CW. Wang et al. [53] adapted CW considering the number of concurrent transmitting vehicles, packet size, length of distributed coordination function inter-frame Space (DIFS), optimal transmission probability and proportion of busy channel time. However, all of these works are proposed in non-clustering scenarios where each vehicle operates and broadcasts independently. In this work, we incorporate dynamic CW in clustering environment where we adapt CW of CMs based on their speed, position and CFS.

2.3 System Model and Proposed CFS based Dynamic Clustering

In this section, we present a system model and our approach to calculate a CFS for each vehicle considering behavioral metrics and a current journey metric. In any cluster, a CM with the highest CFS is elected as a CH. Parameters used to calculate CFS are shown in Table 2.1. The CH then creates a cluster table (as shown in Fig. 2.1) by grouping CMs according to the direction to follow after the upcoming intersection or highway exits. The usual directions to follow are take exit left or take exit right or keep on driving on the road. The cluster table (Fig. 2.1) facilitates easy partitioning into sub-clusters and merging of sub-clusters which is mostly required after crossing an intersection. Once a cluster is formed, the coordination inside the cluster is fully managed by a CH.

Table 2.1 Parameters for calculating CFS

Symbols	Definitions
D_T	Total distance traveled by a vehicle
D_{TC}	Total distance traveled by a vehicle with cluster
N_{DC}	Total count of cluster disconnection
D_{CD}	Distance to travel in current direction before taking exit
τ	Trust level of a vehicle

Using the parameters specified in Table 2.1, CFS is calculated with following expression.

$$CFS = \left(\frac{D_{TC}}{\sqrt{D_T}} \times \frac{1}{\exp^{K_1 \times \frac{N_{DC}}{D_T}}} + K_2 \times \sqrt{D_{CD}} \right) \times \tau \qquad (2.1)$$

In the Equation 2.1, D_T represents the total distance that a vehicle has driven till current time. whereas, D_{TC} represents total distance that a vehicle has driven being associated with cluster.

Higher value of $\frac{D_{TC}}{\sqrt{D_T}}$ means that a vehicle traveled associating with cluster most of the time. We used $\sqrt{D_T}$ instead of D_T to control the rise of CFS for vehicles with shorter travel history. For realizing a stable cluster, a vehicle is expected to be associated with a cluster while traveling. However, a vehicle may leave a cluster opportunistically and such act should be penalized. For this N_{DC} stores total disconnection count and the term $\frac{1}{\exp K1 \times \frac{N_{DC}}{D_T}}$ penalizes each vehicle by reducing CFS for significant disconnection. A constant K_1 is used to vary the reduction factor. D_{CD} is used to prioritize a vehicle in the current direction to be selected as a CH. Constant K2 controls the priority. τ has a significant role in the value of CFS. Initially, the value of $\tau=1$ and it decreases gradually with malicious action of a CM and consequently reduces the values of CFS.

Table 2.2 lists symbols with its meaning for cluster table shown in Fig. 2.1. L_{CM} in the Fig. 2.1 represents maximum limit on the number of CMs in a lane. The limit on a lane and a cluster has been derived in Section 2.5. For a cluster, cluster table is created by a CH where some entries are filled by CH while others are filled by CMs itself.

Table 2.2 Cluster table entries

Symbols	Definitions
V_{ID}	Vehicle ID
τ	Trust level of a vehicle
CFS	Cluster fitness score of a vehicle
$V_{C,GPS}$	Vehicle's current GPS
$V_{D,GPS}$	Vehicle's destination GPS
S_V	Speed of a vehicle
T_{EX}	Timer expiration
CH_{ID}	Cluster head ID
$CH_{isRechable}$	Is CH reachable
C_{Mode}	Communication mode

To build a stable cluster, a trust factor is used. If a malicious vehicle joins a cluster, it might forge and/or broadcast fake message(s). Such activity is monitored in the cluster and accordingly trust factor is updated. A message might be changed because of low signal-to-noise-ratio (SNR). So, we also consider this using threshold of SNR with probability of error. Let, $\zeta_{CM[i]}$ be the instantaneous SNR of ith CM and $\bar{\zeta}_{CM[i]}$ be the minimum threshold, then a probability of error is

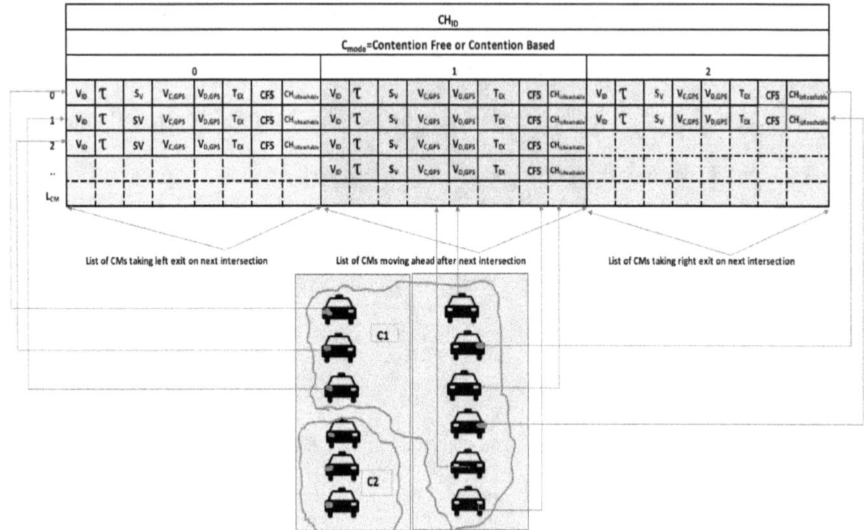

Figure 2.1. Cluster table for cluster C1

computed as,

$$P_{\zeta_{CM[i]}}(t) = Pr(\zeta_{CM[i]} < \bar{\zeta}_{CM[i]}) = 1 - Pr(\zeta_{CM[i]} \geq \bar{\zeta}_{CM[i]}) \tag{2.2}$$

Now, we define whether a CM is malicious or legitimate based on its suspicion level by using the Bayesian criterion. For an observation period θ_t, suspicion level for a CM is,

$$\alpha_{CM[i]}(t) = \frac{P(\theta_t|CM[i]_m = M)P(CM[i]_m = M)}{\sum_{i=1}^{N} P(\theta_t|CM[i]_h = M)P(CM[i]_h = M))} \tag{2.3}$$

where, N is the number of CMs and $CM[i]_m$ and $CM[i]_h$ represent malicious CM 'M' or honest CM 'H' respectively. Furthermore, we combine equations 2.2 and 2.3 and define suspicion level caused by low SNR and deliberate change of message as,

$$\alpha_{CM[i]}(t, \zeta_{CM[i]}) = P_{\zeta_{CM[i]}}(t) \times \alpha_{CM[i]}(t) \tag{2.4}$$

Finally, we compute trust level of an ith CM using suspicion level and considering the number of received messages as,

$$\tau(t, \zeta_{CM[i]}) = \frac{1 - \alpha_{CM[i]}(t, \zeta_{CM[i]})}{|E_m|} \tag{2.5}$$

where, $|E_m|$ is the number of received messages for observation period θ_t. τ for each CM is ultimately stored in the cluster table as $\frac{\sum_{N-1} \tau(t, \zeta_{CM[i]})}{N-1}$, which is the average of the trust value of other N-1 CMs for i^{th} CM. This trust value is used to calculate CFS for every CM including CH. If a CH shows malicious behavior, its CFS is decreased accordingly and another CM with higher score is elected as a CH.

2.4 Cluster Formation and Cluster Management

A cluster formation starts with sending cluster join request (joinCR) by a vehicle or non-cluster member (NCM) to another nearby vehicle. When a NCM sends joinCR, it specifies its ID, CFS, speed, current GPS, and destination GPS. If the nearby vehicle agrees to form a cluster, it acknowledges by creating a cluster table, filling the necessary information, and broadcasting it to the requester. If there is already an existing cluster nearby, the vehicle sends joinCR to the CH. A NCM may choose a suitable cluster based on the information it received from the nearby clusters. It then fills the entries of the vehicle in a particular cell of the existing cluster table according to its destination. In a cluster, a CH is selected by initializing CH_{ID} field with the ID of a CM with the highest CFS. The cluster table is then broadcasted to all the CMs.

The cluster keeps on expanding when non-cluster members(NCMs) keep joining the cluster. The continuation of this process depends on the number of CMs in a cluster. In a cluster table, CH groups CMs as sub-clusters according to directions to follow to facilitate easy partition after the intersection. After partition, each sub-cluster becomes a cluster, and a CM with the highest CFS acts as CH. Different sub-clusters if moving in the same direction, are merged to form a single cluster. If the merging sub-cluster exceeds the limit on the number of CMs, entries of CMs with lower scores are removed from the cluster table. These excluded vehicles restart clustering process again.

In a cluster, each CM works on its own to maintain its map, lane, speed, velocity, and acceleration. Almost all the communications between CH, CMs, and other parties take place using DSRC standard except a few unicast and geocast. However, the communications that are supposed to be originated from a cluster are supervised by the CH. CH coordinates these communications to allow CMs to exchange BSM and non-BSM messages respectively. Each CM broadcasts its BSM periodically in contention free communication (CFC) and broadcasts other messages in contention-based communication (CBC) supervised by CH. For contention free communications, CH assigns a timer to each CM in the corresponding entry of the cluster table. This is required to schedule each CM when to broadcast its BSM frames without contention. However, the value of the timer may change depending on scenarios like a change in the number of CMs or change in the average speed of the cluster. CH notifies CMs about this by broadcasting the cluster table. When the timer of a particular CM expires, it immediately broadcasts its frame where the range of the broadcast is determined as per the extreme positions of CMs. The timer value is assigned such that each CM broadcasts its BSM within 100 ms. Apart from other messages, CH also broadcasts its BSM periodically. With this, each CM identifies whether the CH is reachable (still in the cluster) or not. CH may update timer value at any time as per the needs. CH also broadcasts any important messages to its cluster when received from outside the cluster. Apart from these, CH might broadcast additional cluster management information independently or piggybacking to other non-BSM messages. The additional information might be the next mode of communication or change in timer value or any important updates. CFC is followed by CBC in an alternate fashion. CBC is necessary to communicate with other communicating parties like RSUs, other CHs, or other vehicles and also to allow CMs to send non-BSM messages. In this mode of communication, CMs need to contend to grab the channel. In a cluster, a CH or any CM may leave a cluster intentionally or unintentionally. Here, we discuss such different issues and present how cluster management is performed to tackle those.

When a CM is out of reach of a cluster: A CM might be out of reach to CH only or to every member of the cluster. In such cases, the CM will not receive any communication from CH. However, it still broadcasts its BSM when its timer expires, but before broadcasting, it updates CH as unreachable in the cluster table. Here, unreachability might be because of two reasons. One is CH or CM might have left the cluster and the other is CH or CM is momentarily out of range because of some change in position, packet collision, channel fading, or others. Sometimes, it might be the case that a CM did not receive a broadcast from CH but CH might still receive a broadcast from that CM. In such a case, a CM figures it out when it finds its updated status in the cluster table when it receives the broadcasts from other CMs. However, if CH did not receive periodic broadcasts from any CM, it removes the entry for that CM to eliminate it from the cluster. If a CM finds its elimination from the cluster table, then the CM acts like an independent vehicle and tries to associate with a suitable cluster. The disconnection counter of this CM gets incremented by the onboard unit (OBU). Similarly, from the moment of CM's association with the cluster till the disconnection, OBU stores the cumulative mileage for the CM. In case of every member out of reach to the CM, it does not receive any broadcasts from any of the CMs. In such a situation, it waits till the expiration of timers of all the CMs in its cluster table and then acts as an independent vehicle.

When multiple CMs are out of reach of a cluster: It is possible that some CMs are out of reach to other CMs as well as to CH. Let us call these two groups as A and B respectively. In such a case, CMs of group A will not receive any broadcast from CH. However, these CMs broadcast their frames when their corresponding timer reaches 0 and mark CH as unreachable. The timer would have been reset by CH if CH was not out of reach. CMs of group A only receive broadcasts from themselves. These CMs are able to update their status but that is within the group only. However, the table is not updated for CMs of group B. When the timer of all the CMs of A reaches 0, these CMs who have marked CH as unreachable, will form a different cluster. Although the timer values of CMs of B also reach 0 in the cluster table of A, there will be no update on the reachability of CH. It might be also possible that at some instance, a CM from B (which was previously out of reach to A) might come to the range of A. In this case, CMs of A will receive the broadcast from this CM but the entries for CMs of A will have already been eliminated from the cluster table. In this case, CMs of A will identify explicitly about their exclusion from the cluster. The CMs of A will then form a cluster and a CM with the highest CFS acts as a CH. The newly elected CH eliminates the entries of CMs of B from the cluster table maintaining by A.

When CH is out of reach of all CMs: When CH leaves the existing cluster and is out of range to any of the CMs, CMs and CH act differently. In the case of CMs, they broadcast their frames according to their respective timer values and mark CH unreachable. Additionally, it is still unknown to all the CMs whether CH has excluded them from the cluster table or not. So, after a complete cycle of broadcasts which is when every CM marks CH as unreachable, a new cluster is formed. A CM with the highest CFS among the group updates CH_{ID} in the current cluster table with its own ID. It then eliminates earlier CH's entry from the table, sets timers and other necessary parameters in the table and broadcasts into the cluster. In another scenario, when CH leaves the cluster, it won't hear the broadcast from any of the CMs. So, it eliminates each CM gradually from the cluster table. When the CM list is empty, it starts to act as an independent vehicle. In such a case, CH is penalized heavily for disconnection.

2.4.1   Calculating Transmission Range for Cluster Members

Here, we devise transmission range (TR) for a CM considering the extreme positions in a cluster. The objective for this is to reduce interference of one cluster to others. Let, N is number of CMs in a cluster. TR is calculated from GPS coordinates of leading CM, trailing CM and the coordinate of ith CM using haversine formula [54] for great circle distance. Let, ϕ_l, ϕ_t and ϕ_i are the latitudes of leading CM, trailing CM and i^{th} CM and λ_l, λ_r and λ_i are the longitudes (latitude and longitude are in radian) of leading CM, trailing CM and i^{th} CM respectively.

Now, the distance between leading and i^{th} CM is,

$$D_{l,i} = 2 \times R \times \sin^{-1} \sqrt{sin^2(\tfrac{\phi_l - \phi_i}{2}) + cos(\phi_l) \times cos(\phi_i) \times sin^2(\tfrac{\lambda_l - \lambda_i}{2})}$$

Where, E_R is earth radius and its value is 6371×10^3 meter.

Similarly, distance between i^{th} and trailing CM is ,

$$D_{i,t} = 2 \times R \times \sin^{-1} \sqrt{sin^2(\frac{\phi_i - \phi_r}{2}) + cos(\phi_i) \times cos(\phi_t) \times sin^2(\frac{\lambda_i - \lambda_t}{2})}$$

Now, transmission range (in meter) for i^{th} CM is,

$TR_i = max(D_{l,i}, D_{i,t})$ and each CM adjusts its power while broadcasting its frame to cover transmission range of TR_i.

2.5 Contention Free and Contention-Based Communication

As mentioned in the previous section, once a cluster is formed, an elected CH supervises contention free and contention-based communications for its cluster members. To improve the IoV performance, a CH may arrange varying number of CFC and CBC slots for its CMs. The number of CMs is an important information to be considered while arranging such slots. A CH could handle only limited number of CMs due to periodic BSM broadcast requirement and transmission range of DSRC. In this section, firstly, we derive a limit on the number of CMs as per our proposed criteria. We then present our contention window adaptation approach and finally, we discuss the allocation of CFC and CBC.

2.5.1 Finding a limit on the number of cluster members

We first find the maximum number of CMs that a cluster can have and then taking the transmission range into account, we also find the maximum number of CMs that can be in a single lane.

We calculate limit considering time required to arrange one CFC is followed by 1 CBC. One CFC is used to allow one CM to broadcast its BSM. After this, CH broadcasts a frame to its cluster. The frame may contain a BSM of CH, any traffic update, cluster management information, or any important message. After this, CH arranges one CBC to allow a CM broadcast its non-BSM frame. In CFC, CH provides timer value based on the cluster information and information received from other nearby communicating parties. So, when timer expires, each CM waits only for short inter frame space (SIFS) time before broadcasting its BSM. After this, each communicating party waits for DIFS time followed by an additional contention window before a winner broadcasts a non-BSM frame. Finally, CH may broadcast any important frame before repeating the communication cycle. We further assume that a propagation delay is associated with every broadcast from any of the communicating parties. In CFC, we assumed saturated traffic condition which means there is always a BSM frame ready to broadcast before timer expiration. However, in CBC, each station contends internally for frames having different ACs (as shown in Table 2.3) before transmitting. The frame with lowest Arbitrary Interframe Spacing (AIFS) or highest priority (if AIFSs are equal for more than one ACs) is transmitted when a station wins the contention.

Now, we derive and calculate total estimated communication time to execute one combined CFC and CBC based on the parameters and values presented in Table. 2.3 and 2.4 as,

$$T_{(t,CFC+CBC)} = SIFS + T_{xf} + \delta + SIFS + T_{xnf} + \delta + DIFS + \sigma \times CW + T_{xnf} + \delta + SIFS + T_{xnf} + \delta$$

Table 2.3 Default EDCA parameters and their value in 802.11p [10] [28]

Access Category(AC)	Frame Types	CW_{min}	CW_{max}	AIFSN [AC]	Frame Size
3	AC_BK	15	1023	9	160 bytes
2	AC_BE	7	15	6	256 bytes
1	AC_VI	3	7	3	200 bytes
0	AC_VO	3	7	2	200 bytes

Table 2.4 Parameter setting

Description	Symbol	Value	Unit
Propagation delay	δ	2	μs
Slot time	σ	13	μs
Short Inter Frame Space	$SIFS$	32	μs
DCF Inter Frame Space	$DIFS$	58	μs
Transmission rate	T_{xr}	3	$Mbps$
BSM Frame Size	F_{BS}	300	$Bytes$
Non-BSM broadcast frame size	F_{NBS}	450	$Bytes$
Transmission time for a BSM frame	T_{xf}	$\frac{F_{BS}}{T_{xr}} = 800$	μs
Transmission time for a non-BSM frame	T_{xnf}	$\frac{F_{NBS}}{T_{xr}} = 1200$	μs

In Table 2.4, we assume a BSM and a non-BSM frame size higher than the value as specified in 802.11p (as shown in Table 2.3). Although, the transmission rate in 802.11p has a range of 3-27 Mbps, we consider the lower value of the range i.e., 3Mbps.

Value of CW for CBC has been taken as maximum CW_{min} value of the lowest priority traffic. We assign extreme values to the parameters to observe the maximum time required for one complete CFC and CBC communication.

Now, we put the values of the parameters to calculate total time $T_{(t,CFC+CBC)}$ as,

$$T_{(t,CFC+CBC)} = 32+800+2+32+1200+2+58+13 \times 15+1200+2+32+1200+2 =\approx 4757 \mu s.$$

Before the same CM broadcasts BSM in 100 ms, $\frac{100 \times 1000}{4757} \approx 21$ such CFC and CBC can happen that means a CH can handle a cluster of 21 CMs efficiently.

We now find a limit on the number of CMs considering the transmission range of DSRC technology (1000 meter) and safe distance between vehicles. We consider maximum allowed speed as 85 miles/hour (mph). Using 4 second rule, the safe distance between vehicles is approximately 500 feet (ft) . Considering maximum allowed speed, within 1000 meter maintaining safe distance of 500 ft (at maximum speed) and taking average length of vehicle as 20 ft, there can be $\frac{1000 \times 3.28084 - 250 - 250}{520} = 5.34$ number of vehicles in a lane. Here, we subtract 500 ft from total range to maintain the gap of 500 ft with the vehicles of leading and trailing cluster. Although, the transmission range for DSRC is 1000 m, to reduce interference with other cluster we limit the number of vehicles to 5 vehicles per lane. The transmission range between leading and trailing vehicle in this scenario will be ≈ 634 m. Here, we limit the number of vehicles only by distance not lane.

2.5.2 Dynamic Contention Window Size for Cluster Members

Here, we devise expression to assign contention window size for each CM to participate in contention-based communication. When CH announces the communication mode as CBC, all the CMs, other CHs, RSUs and NCMs contend for the channel access. For the proposed approach, the contention window size for non-cluster parties will be according to default standard whereas that for CMs will be relatively higher. Doing so enables non-cluster parties higher chance to grab the channel. The additional size of CW for a CM depends on its speed, position and CFS score as shown below,

$$CW[i]_{CM} = [0 - CW_{min}] + \left\lceil \left(K3 \times \frac{S_{Max}}{(S[i]_{CM}+1)} + K4 \times \frac{TR_{Max}}{CH_P - CM[i]_P} \right) \times \frac{1}{CFS[i]_{CM}} \right\rceil$$

Where, $CW[i]_{CM}$ represents contention window of a CM,

$S[i]_{CM}$ represents current speed of a CM,

S_{Max} represents maximum allowed speed,

CH_P represents GPS location of CH,

$CM[i]_P$ represents GPS location of a CM, and

TR_{Max} represents maximum distance between any two CM

$CFS[i]_{CM}$ represents CFS of a CM.

In the above expression, $\frac{S_{Max}}{(S[i]_{CM}+1)}$ increases with decrease in speed of CM. It signifies that when CMs are moving slow in high traffic scenario, CW of CMs is further increased to reduce the channel contention.

Similarly, $\frac{TR_{Max}}{CH_P-CM[i]_P}$ increases with decrease in distance between CH and CM. It prioritizes a CM which is farther from CH with shorter contention window among its peers.

Finally, the term $\frac{1}{CFS[i]_{CM}}$ also contributes to increase in CW with decrease in CFS. This allows a CM with higher CFS an opportunity to grab the channel earlier. Finally, with different values of constants K3 and K4, we can control increase in contention window size of CMs.

2.5.3 Allocation of Contention Free and Contention-Based Communication Slots

In a cluster, CH supervises communication where each CFC is followed by a CBC. However, to improve IoV performance, a CH may vary this as per the changing speed and number of CMs. For example, in a traffic jam scenario, when vehicles of a cluster are not moving, it is not necessary to allow CFC to CMs frequently. In such a case, it is better to communicate more outside the cluster. So, instead of following one CFC slot by one CBC slot, allocating a greater number of CBC slots would be better. Similarly, if the number of CMs in a cluster is low, one CFC followed by one CBC may allow each CM to broadcast its BSM so frequently that a new frame might not have been even generated for a CM to broadcast. In both cases, it is better to allocate a greater number of CBC slots so that communicating parties outside the cluster get more chance to broadcast its frame. In other cases, when the average speed of a cluster is high and the number of CMs is high, it is better to allow CMs to broadcast frequently by reducing CBC frequency. The change in CFC and CBC frequencies is also beneficial when a highway has a high number of lanes. As mentioned in Section 2.5.1, each lane can have a maximum of 5 CMs and the total limit on the number of CMs is 20. But, when the number of lanes is quite high, there might be more than one cluster quite near to each other traveling in the same direction which is likely to increases the network congestion and interference. However, by increasing CFC slots by reducing CBC slots, we can mitigate such problems. By doing so, a CH can accommodate a greater number of CMs to reduce the chance of the presence of another cluster nearby. With this approach, a CH can have twice the maximum number of CMs that can be in a cluster. However, when CH accommodates this number, it cannot arrange any CBC. To overcome this, we allow the growth of CMs to a maximum of $\frac{3}{4} \times 2L_{CM}$ so that CMs get chance to broadcast non-BSM messages.

Now, we derive the distribution of CFC and CBC slots with respect to change in speed and the number of CMs. Let us consider that $\bar{S}$ is the maximum allowed speed, $S_M = \frac{\bar{S}}{2}$ is the mean speed, S_{Avg} is the current average speed of a cluster, N_{CM} is the current number of cluster members in a cluster, and $\bar{N}_{CM}$ is the limit on number of CMs in 4 lanes scenario.

$\hat{N}_{CM} = \frac{3}{4} \times 2\bar{N}_{CM}$ is the maximum number of CMs for greater than 4 lanes scenario. $I_{S,N} = S_M \times \bar{N}_{CM}$ is the product of speed and number of CMs for which one CFC is followed by 1 CBC.

For $i = 0$ to $(\bar{S} \times \hat{N}_{CM})$

$$CFC[i+1] = \min(L, \max(1, 1 + \lfloor \tfrac{(i-I_{S,N})^3}{K5} \rfloor))) \ CBC[i+1] = \min(L, \max(1, 1 - \lfloor \tfrac{(i-I_{S,N})^3}{K6} \rfloor))$$

where, i represents possible values of the products of $S_{Avg} \times N_{CM}$, L represents a limit for CFC and CBC slots. and $CFC[i+1]$ and $CBC[i+1]$ represent the dynamic slots for different combination of average cluster speed and number of CMs.

2.6 Reward Model for Cluster Head and Members

The main objective of the proposed reward model is to form stable clusters by encouraging each vehicle to be associated with a cluster without unnecessary disconnection. For malicious activities as well as frequent disconnections, CMs (including CH) are penalized by decreasing CFS. Whereas if a CM maintains its high CFS with good acts, the contention window size is lowered as per its score. With a smaller contention window, a vehicle gets the priority for winning the channel and making required communication. Any CM always gets the chance to broadcast its BSM in CFC mode while a CM with a higher score has a higher chance to communicate in CBC than other CMs. With this privilege, such CMs can utilize CBC to know traffic updates, parking information, local geographical information, and so on earlier than other CMs. Furthermore, when a CM with s highest CFS elected as CH, it gets more chance to access communication channel compared to other communicating parties (as explained in Section 2.5.1). So, our proposed model encourages each vehicle to increase its CFS by maintaining good acts and also get a chance to be elected as a CH.

2.7 Performance Evaluation and Analysis

The main motive of this research is to form stable clusters that improve IoV's network performances. To observe the stability and network performances, we performed independent simulations in slightly different setups. We discuss a common setup for these simulations in the next paragraph followed by their differences in respective subsections. The cluster stability performance of the proposed approach is compared with SCalE [36] method whereas IoV's network performance is compared with the default approach (802.11p). We chose SCalE for comparison as it demonstrated well to build stable clusters and furthermore, the metrics we chose to form clusters closely match with SCalE. Unlike SCalE, our work incorporates past behaviors, trust factor and distance to travel in current direction as additional metrics than SCalE.

For the common simulation set up, we chose a highway scenario of 4 one-way lanes where we distributed 200 vehicles randomly and assigned positions to them considering minimum safe distance plus a random value between 1 to 150. Velocity to each vehicle was assigned randomly between 45 to 70 miles/hour. To calculate CFS, parameters' values were assigned as per the Table 2.5. Initially, we assigned trust level value 1 to all vehicles. Later, we selected 1 to $\frac{1}{10}$ of total vehicles randomly as malicious and assigned trust level value between 0 to 1. This affects the CFS of vehicles and which may change CH of any cluster accordingly. Values to constants K1 and K2 were assigned as 1.

Proposed approach was implemented to form different number of clusters by sending cluster join requests. In this process, different clusters may merge to form a single cluster, a CH or CM may leave a cluster and the cluster management is performed accordingly. The simulations were carried out for a total duration of 200s.

2.7.1 Cluster Stability Performance Analysis

We implemented the proposed approach and SCalE algorithm in our simulation setup to compare the cluster stability performance. To compare, we considered average CM lifetime and number of CH re-elections as performance metrics. CM lifetime measures the time a vehicle associates with the same cluster and the number of CH re-elections measures the number of new CH elections when CH goes out of transmission range. These two are significantly important metrics to measure the stability of clusters. For comparison, number of CH re-elections is normalized by the highest value. To create a similar scenario and compare the results with SCalE, we placed an exit at the highway. We assigned the distance to travel in the current direction in a way that 20 percent of the total vehicles leave at the exit when they travel 3 km from their initial position while the rest will participate throughout the simulation period. During the simulation period, the performance metrics were monitored for transmission ranges (TRs) 300, 600 and 900 meters which are plotted as shown in Fig. 2.2 and Fig. 2.3.

Fig. 2.2 shows the number of CH re-elections decreases in both approaches however, the proposed approach shows better performance in all TRs. It is because the proposed approach also considers distance to travel in the current direction when electing a CH. So, it is less likely that CHs leave clusters at the exit and the corresponding re-elections are required. In Fig. 2.3, average CM lifetime in both the approaches is similar at lower transmission range, however, when transmission range is higher, the proposed approach demonstrates better results. In the proposed approach, a

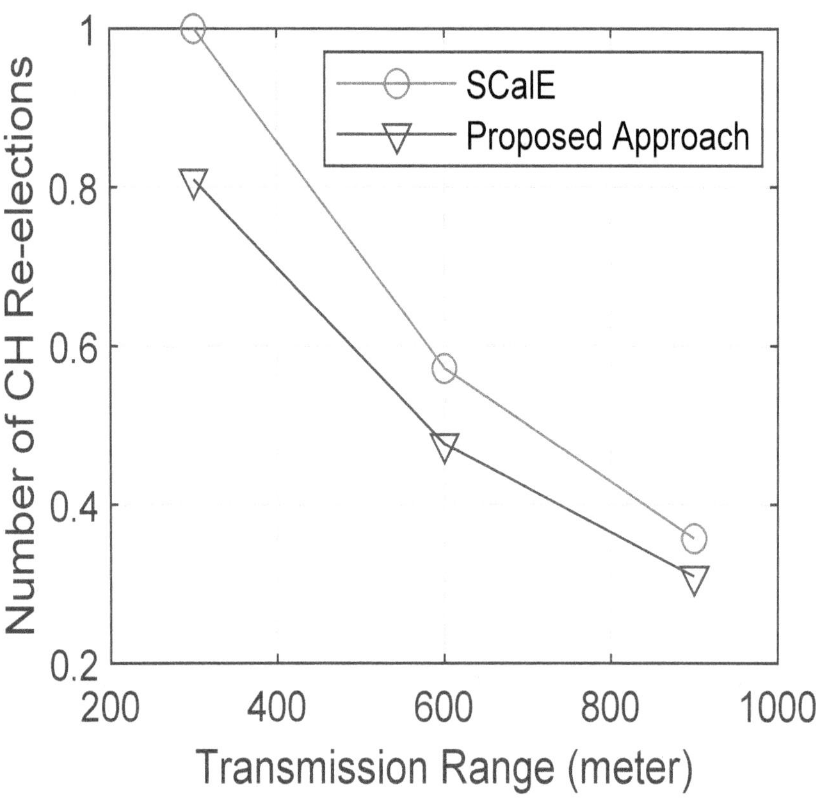

Figure 2.2. Comparison of the proposed approach with SCalE [36] for normalized average number of CH re-elections.

CM or a CH may be momentarily out of range and which is handled without re-affiliation or re-election. Furthermore, if a CH is out-of-range, a CM with the highest CFS from the remaining CMs is chosen as CH. As a result, CMs need not go through re-affiliations which increases the lifetime of a CM with the same cluster. For comparison, we presented the results for different TRs however, in the proposed approach, CM or CH adjusts TR based on the positional information of the cluster, which enhances the coverage and reduces the detachment of CM or CH.

2.7.2 <u>IoV's Network Performance Analysis</u>

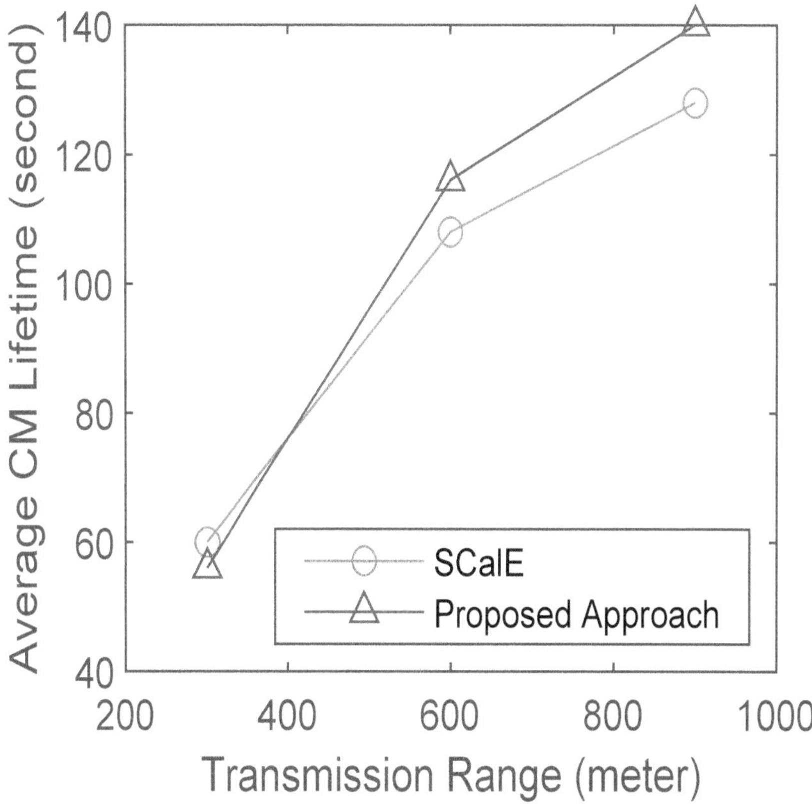

Figure 2.3. Comparison of the proposed approach with SCalE [36] for average CM lifetime.

To measure IoV's network performance (in terms of delivery, collision and dropping of frames), we set additional required parameters' values as specified in Table 2.3 and Table 2.4. The packets that arrive in the media access control (MAC) layer were generated following a Poisson distribution of 10 packets/second. CW size for a non-bsm frame was set dynamically as specified in Section 2.5.2. The constant values for K3 and K4 were chosen as 2 and 3 respectively. For simplicity, we ignored internal collision in the MAC layer. The retry limit for each frame before dropping was assigned a random value between 1 to 10 and the back-off principle was implemented as specified in 802.11p. We also neglected propagation delay and channel properties to keep it simple. Finally, we removed the exit in the highway to let all the vehicles participate for entire simulation period. During the simulation period, values for the performance metrics were recorded for both clustering and default approaches.

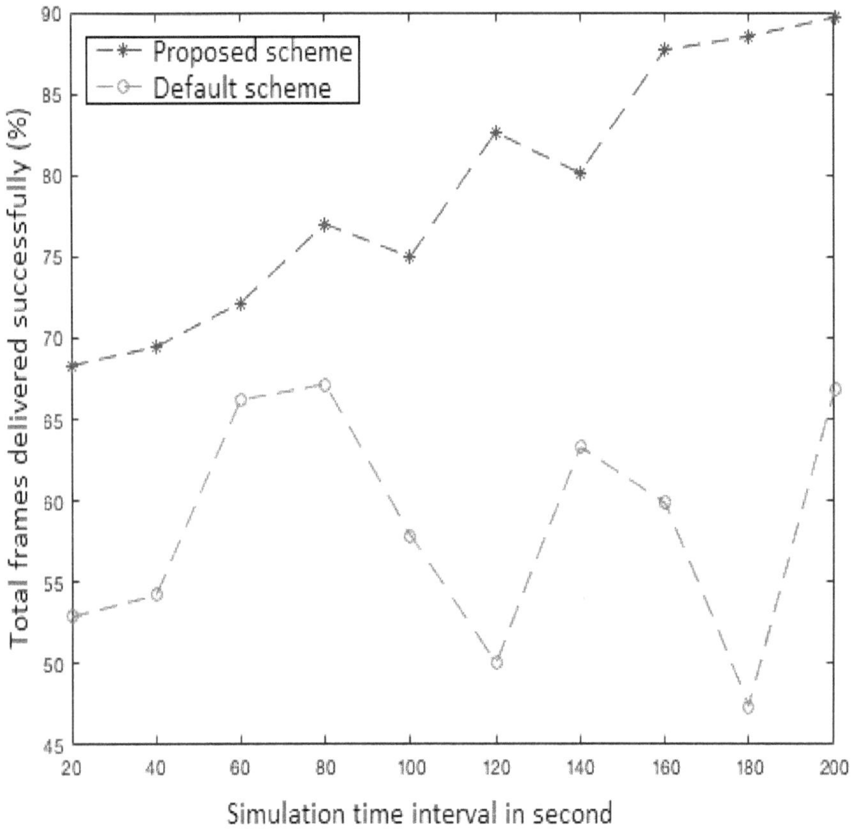

Figure 2.4. Percentage of frames delivered successfully vs simulation time

Comparison of total frames delivered successfully in clustered approach and default approach is shown in Fig. 2.4. As we can see, cluster approach clearly outperformed default approach throughout the simulation period because CH in each cluster coordinates communication based on the information of nearby clusters and its CMs. We observed similar results regarding frames' collision in both approaches as shown in Fig. 2.5. With the increase in number of clusters formed, percentage of frames collision reduced significantly in proposed approach. In the case of frames' drop, we observed a low percentage of drop for both approaches. However, the proposed approach performed better throughout the simulation period as shown in Fig. 2.6. This is mainly due to the

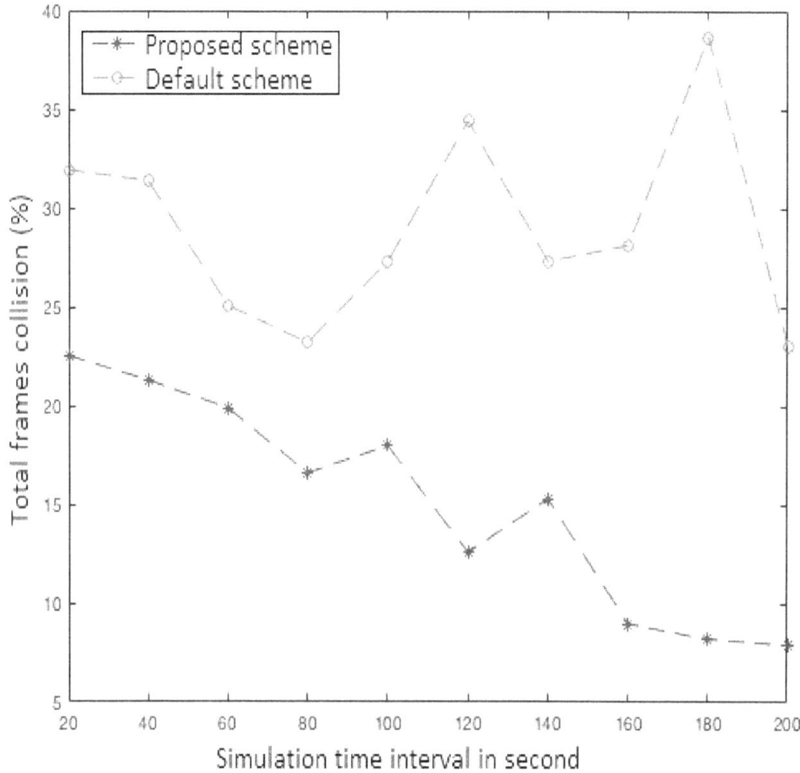

Figure 2.5. Percentage of frames experienced collision vs simulation time

reduction in channel contention between communicating parties by the use of dynamic CW.

2.7.3 Simulation of dynamic allocation of CFC and CBC slots

For the simulation of dynamic allocation of CFC and CBC slots as specified in Section 2.5.3, we set maximum speed as 100 $miles/hour$ and maximum number of CMs as 30 which is $\frac{3}{4} \times 2N_{CM}$. Values for constants are set as $K5 = 10^7$ and $K6 = 10^7$ respectively. We set maximum limit on CBC and CFC slots in the simulation as maximum possible number of CMs which is 30.

Values of CFC and CBC slots are plotted against the speed, number of CMs and its products. When speed is 50 $miles/hour$ and the number of CMs is 20, one CFC is followed by one CBC. But, when the product of speed and number of CMs is greater than 50×20, number of CFC slots

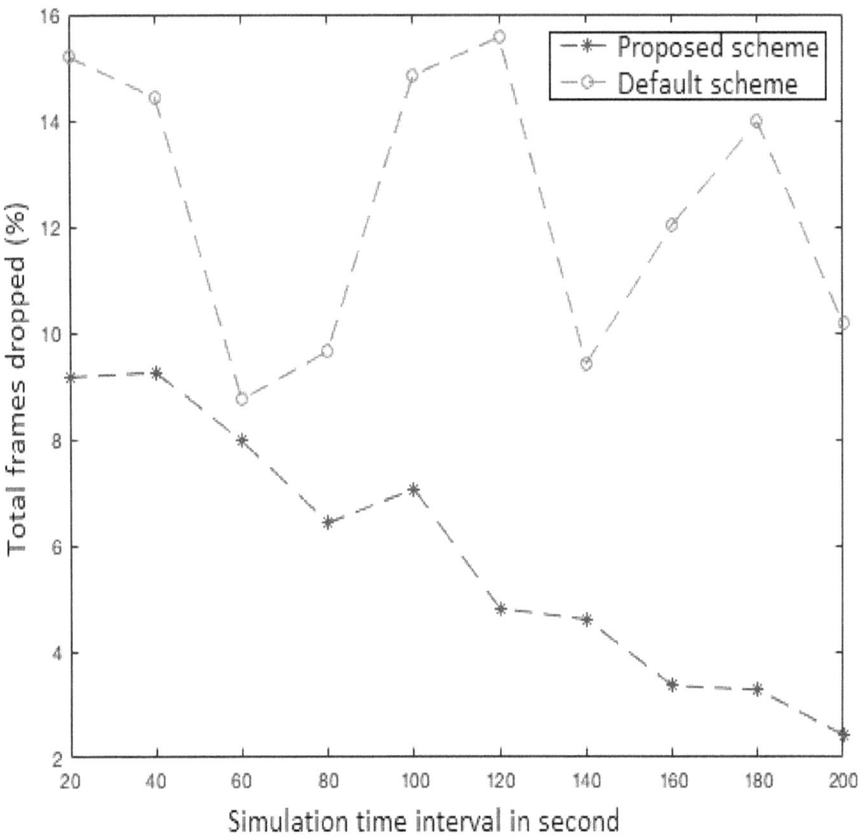

Figure 2.6. Percentage of frames dropped vs simulation time

increases otherwise number of CBC increases. For example, if CFC is 15 that means 15 continuous

CFC is followed by one CBC where as if CBC is 15, 1 CFC is followed by 15 CBC. The simulation

results of expression of Section 2.5.3 are shown in Figures 2.7, 2.8, and 2.9. Figure 2.7 illustrates

that when the product of the average speed of the cluster is equal to 50×20, one CFC is followed

by 1 CBC. whereas if the product is less than 50×20, CBC slots increase with keeping the value

of CFC 1.

Table 2.5 Values of parameters for IoV simulation

Symbols	Definitions	Value Range
D_T	Total distance traveled by a vehicle	0 to 200000
D_{TC}	Total distance traveled by a vehicle with cluster	0 to D_T
N_{DC}	Total count of cluster disconnection	0 to D_T
τ	Trust level of a vehicle	0 to 1
$D_{NCM,CH[i]}$	Distance between NCM to a CH	150 m to 1000 m
$\bar{L}_{CM}$	Maximum limit on number of cluster members in a cluster	20
$T[i]_{CM}$	Total number of clusters members in a cluster	2 to $\bar{L}_{CM}$

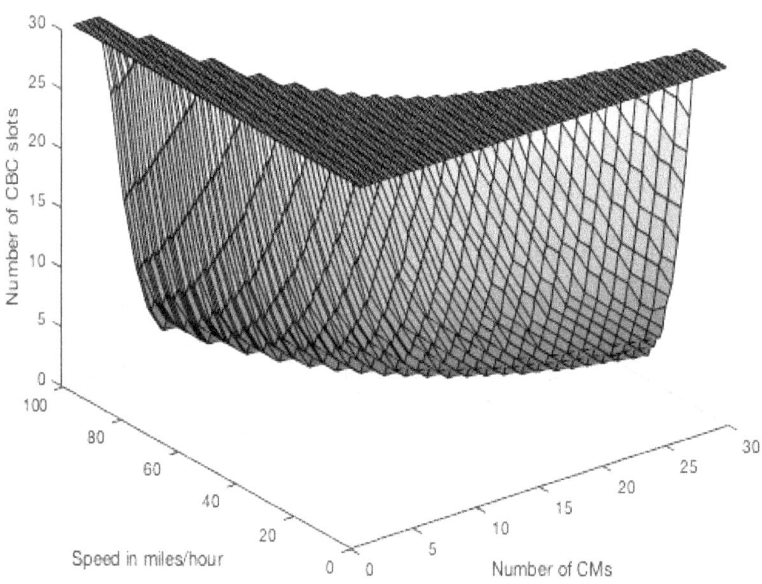

Figure 2.9. Change in CBC as per the average speed of the cluster and the number of CMs

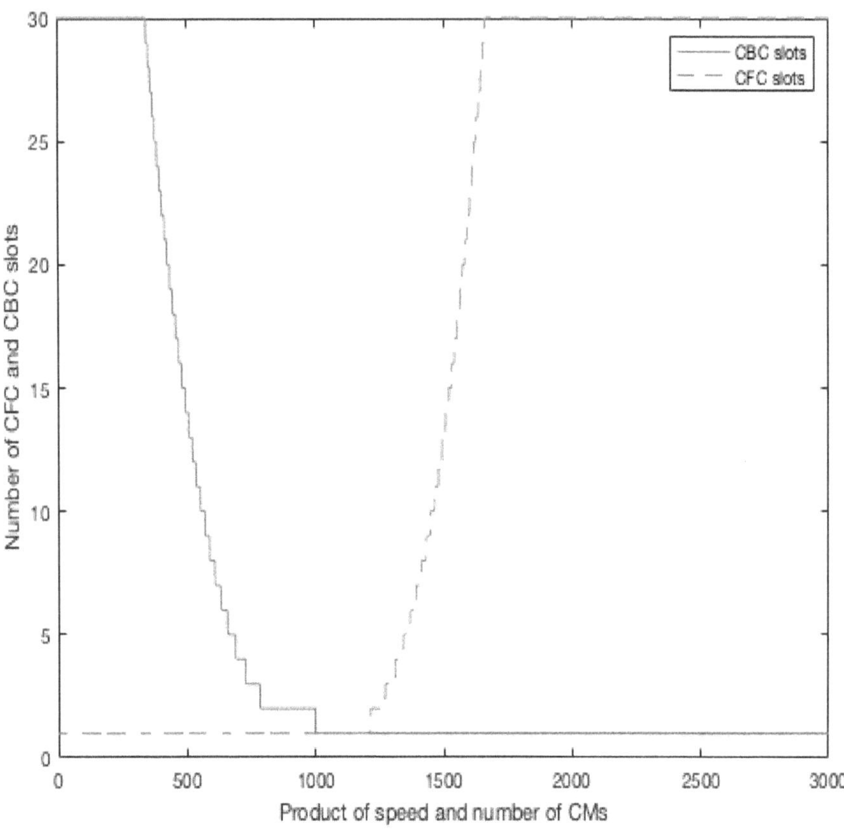

Figure 2.7. Change in CFC and CBC slots as per product of average speed of cluster and number of CMs

This means, at lower speed and lesser number of CMs, CH allows CMs to broadcast less frequently and communicates more outside. This rate of increase in CBC rises with the decrease in the product of speed and number of CMs before reaching a limit value. However, increase rate of CFC rises with the increase in the product above 50×20 keeping CBC 1. In this case, CH allows CMs to broadcast more frequently by reducing communication outside the cluster keeping CBC 1. Finally, CFC reaches the limit and remains constant. Figures 2.8 and 2.9 show 3-D plots of CFC and CBC values against the average speed of cluster and the number of CMs.

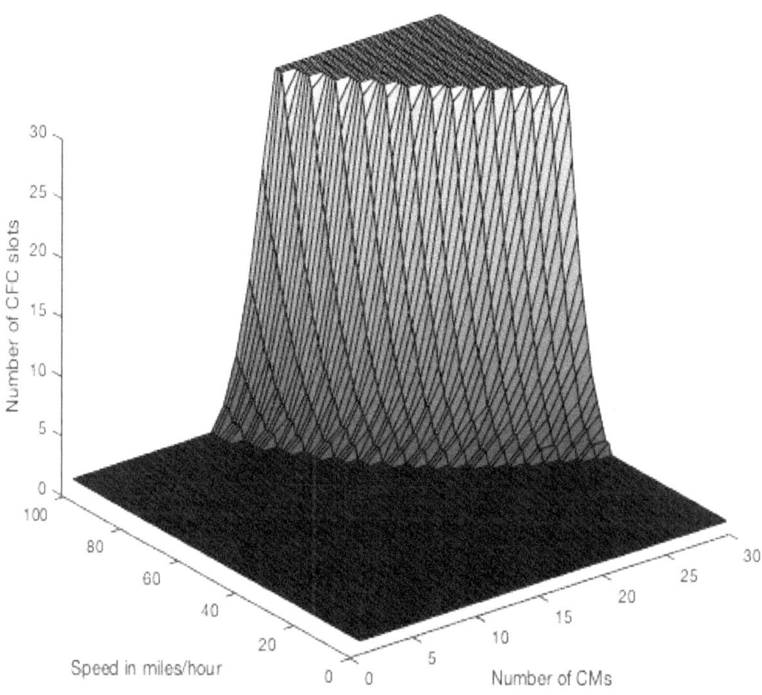

Figure 2.8. Change in CFC as per the average speed of the cluster and the number of CMs

2.8 Chapter Summary

In this paper, we presented a novel clustering approach to form stable clusters by leveraging behavioral and a current journey parameters. We also proposed an approach to adapt contention window size dynamically to enhance the overall network performance. Performance evaluation was carried out using extensive simulations to demonstrate cluster stability and IoV's network performance. We compared the stability results with SCalE algorithm and our approach performed better to enhance number of CH re-elections and average cluster member life. Additionally, we also compared the network performance results with default approach and our approach outperformed it in terms of successful packets delivery, packets collision and packets drop rates. This paper also proposed CH supervised CFC and CBC communication for CMs. Simulation of allocation of CFC and CBC slots according to an average speed of cluster and number of CMs were presented with results. Finally, a reward model concept was also applied on top of clustering to supplement the stability and resiliency of clusters.

CHAPTER 3.   A COMMUNICATION EFFICIENT MACHINE LEARNING FRAMEWORK FOR THE INTERNET OF VEHICLES

3.1   Introduction

The study of Internet of Vehicles to envision as a solution to achieve an intelligent transport system (ITS) has been underway for the past few decades. It is believed that IoV, with the rapid progress in vehicular technologies, communication technologies, smart sensors, machine learning and others, will address current transportation challenges. A vehicle's actions at any given moment are largely determined by the machine learning (ML) algorithm running on it, which processes data obtained from smart sensors such as GPS, RADAR, LiDAR, cameras, and others, as well as data received from other vehicles and infrastructure.

Building ML models from the collaboration of wide spread clients has led to the growth and improvement of various IoT applications and services [1]. Paying attention to the privacy and communication cost, ML architecture involving large amount of wide spread clients is on the verge of transitioning from centralized to federated learning (FL) [55]. However, CL still offers a better accuracy (e.g. [55–57]. When dealing with Non-IID data, stateless and resource-constrained local training in FL, the resulting aggregated global model is expected to be less accurate than in centralized learning [58]. With safety as the top priority, an ML model used in a vehicle must maintain a high level of accuracy and be continuously refined to adapt to changing scenarios over time. However, the sophisticated sensors in the smart vehicles generate a tremendous volume of data at each fraction of time. The transmission of data from all vehicles to a central server could pose a significant communication challenge over the efficient implementation of the centralized learning. Time-sensitive applications and services in IoV could be severely impacted, potentially presenting safety risks [58].

In this regard, we present a novel approach to create a communication efficient centralized learning network by using a sampling strategy to select only the valuable observations without compromising loss in performance. The quality of IoT sensor observations is influenced by several factors such as the quality of the operating environment, communication network and wireless resources, computing resources, battery power, and others. Due to these factors, it's possible that not all vehicles may have valuable data to offer or could negatively impact the learning model. To limit network congestion and create a more efficient communication network, such data can be excluded.

The proposed learning framework includes vehicles transmitting sensors' data to nearby road side infrastructure. The RSI then implements a sampling strategy on the received data and only forwards the valuable data to a centralized server. The number of samples to be selected by the RSI is determined based on the estimated delay from the RSI to the centralized server. This allows the RSI to balance between the amount of data to be transmitted and the delay incurred in transmitting the data to the server. The proposed sampling strategy uses Mahalanobis distance metric to select the observations of interest. The MD measures the multivariate distance between a point and a distribution, providing a measure of how much the point deviates from the mean of the distribution. Vehicles are equipped with varieties of sensors and we assume that in most cases sensors' data naturally are normally distributed. In such scenario, MD could be an effective tool to exploit the multivariate distribution of sensors' data and select valuable observations.

We evaluate the proposed approach by designing a ML task in centralized learning setting. The data sampled by road side infrastructures (RSIs) are collected and used to solve a ML problem. The ML performance of the proposed approach which only make use of sampled data is compared with the ML performance of a standard approach which utilizes all the data. The effectiveness of the proposed approach is verified by training and testing first with synthetic data which follows almost ideal multivariate normal distribution followed by confirming the performance on real dataset consisting of on board diagnostics (OBD) Data.

To the best of our knowledge, no prior studies have attempted to use data sampling approach based on the value of information in it that can handle the high level and that can handle the significant level of proliferation and still perform nearly as considering all available data. Specifically, our contributions include:

1. Presenting a novel approach to use MD metric to sample useful observations.

2. Presenting a sampling strategy where dynamic sampling ratio is applied according to changing network scenario.

3. Presenting a novel approach that offers a high scalability to address possible exponential growth of smart vehicles and its sensors and that without noticeable performance loss.

The rest of the paper is organized as follows. In Section 5.2, the previous efforts aimed at addressing a similar issue are discussed. Section 3.3 presents the background on multivariate normal distribution and MD. Section 5.4 presents the proposed system model and the proposed approach followed by the dataset preparation and simultion setup in Section 3.5. The performance of the proposed approach is evaluated in Section 5.5. Finally, Section 5.6 concludes the paper.

3.2 Related Work

The proliferation of smart vehicles and its sensors could pose the communication overhead to send data vehicles' data to a centralized server and be a bottleneck for system scalability. Sending huge amount of data to a central server can result in substantial traffic congestion and significant communication delays. In literature, authors could not find research that highlight work in CL that offers the potential to reduce communication cost significantly and still exhibits almost the same ML performance as of considering all the data.

One of the main reasons to the emergence of distributed learning (DL) is to address the communication cost to transfer data to a centralized server. Literature extensively covers approaches to reduce communication cost in distributed learning (DL). Various techniques, including compression (such as in [59, 60]), quantization (such as in [61]), clustering (such as in [62, 63]), alternating direction method of multipliers (ADMM) (such as in [64]), learning model partitioning (such as in [65]), and other techniques, have been investigated and tested for their effectiveness in the DL setting. However, some of these techniques (e.g. quantization, ADMM, model partitioning) are specific to DL only while compression can be used in CL as a supplement to further improve communication cost. Several approaches to reduce communication cost in DL setting could result in loss of accuracy [66]. Additionally, this could further increase the safety risks for vehicles.

Numerous studies have examined wireless factors that could influence the communication performance, such as those outlined in [67–70]. However, the proposed approach takes a distinct direction by selecting valuable observations, and these methods can be integrated to enhance overall system performance.

Compared to prior works, the proposed work is a totally different approach to address the communication cost and is highly scalable to address high level of proliferation of smart vehicles and its sensors. We exploit the distribution of sensors' observations in multivariate space and sample the observations to select valuable observations while still ensuring that the sampled observations perform as well as using all available observations.

3.3 Multivariate Normal Distribution and Mahalanobis Distance: Background

The normal distribution is a crucial continuous probability distribution in engineering and science. It is frequently used to model a wide range of real-world phenomena and is often an accurate approximation [5].

Many statistical tests and methods assume that events follow a normal distribution, which has become a popular choice for modeling complex phenomena in simpler models among statisticians [71]. Our proposed approach relies on the assumption that sensory data in vehicles follows a normal distribution to a large extent. We believe that the normal distribution can serve as a reliable approximation, particularly with a large sample size.

In the proposed work, each sensor observation (X_i) in vehicles is assumed to be normally distributed with mean μ and variance σ^2, represented as a probability density function (PDF) $X_i \sim \mathcal{N}(\mu, \sigma^2)$. For a single sensor, the PDF for univariate normal distribution (UVND) can be written as:

$$f(x; \mu, \sigma^2) = \frac{1}{\sqrt{2\pi\sigma^2}} \exp\{-\frac{1}{2\sigma^2}(x - \mu)^2\} \tag{3.1}$$

where, $x \in \mathbb{R}$ represent an observation of a sensor.

By considering the joint distribution of values of several sensors, we can use statistical techniques to classify the different states of vehicles more accurately. Multivariate normal distribution (MVND) is a useful tool for this type of analysis because it takes into account the dependence between the variables, which is important in characterizing complex systems like a network of sensors monitoring vehicle states.

A UVND of sensors' observation have been well applied for several classification problems. However, this paper focuses on a scenario with multiple sensors, where the combined observational values from these sensors are used to classify the different states of vehicles. To do this, we consider the joint distribution of sensors' observations also called as MVND and use statistical technique to classify the different states of vehicles. The MVND is a generalization of the UVND to multiple dimensions to describe the joint distribution of multiple random variables.

The multivariate normal distribution (MVND) holds a significant position in statistics due to its popularity and extensive usage across a broad range of applications. In many instances, inference methods applied to vector-valued data rely on the MVND assumption, making it an appropriate model for addressing numerous real-world issues related to such data.

The MVND is indeed one of the most well-known and widely used distributions in statistics and plays a major role in various areas of applications. Many inference procedures for analyzing vector-valued data are based on the assumption of MVND, making it a suitable model for many real-life problems concerning vector-valued data. The central limit theorem states that even if the original data does not follow a MVND, the MVND can still be used to approximate the distribution of the sample mean vector in the large sample case [72]. The MVND's versatility and applicability in various fields make it a key component in statistical modeling and analysis. The density function of a MVND is fully determined by its mean vector and covariance matrix Σ. The mean vector represents the expected values of the MVND, while the covariance matrix characterizes the relationships between the variables and the amount they vary together [73].

Suppose we have p sensors for each vehicle and we assume that the observations from each sensor $(X_1, X_2, ..., X_p)$ follow a normal distribution. For the MVND, the PDF can be expressed as $X \sim \mathcal{N}(\mu, \Sigma)$.

The joint PDF for p random variables, which represent the observations from p sensors, can be represented as follows:

$$f(x; \mu, \Sigma) = \frac{1}{\sqrt{(2\pi)^p |\Sigma|}} \exp\{-\frac{1}{2}(\mathbf{x} - \mu)^T \Sigma^{-1}(\mathbf{x} - \mu)\} \tag{3.2}$$

In Equation 3.2, $\mathbf{x}$ is a random vector of the observations from the p sensors, μ is the mean vector, Σ is a $p \times p$ covariance matrix, and $|\Sigma|$ is its determinant. The diagonal elements of Σ are the variances of each variable and the off-diagonal elements are the covariances between the variables. Σ^{-1} is the inverse covariance matrix of the independent variables.

In the equation for the UVND (3.1), the argument inside the exponential function $-\frac{1}{2\sigma^2}(x - \mu)^2$ is a quadratic function of the variable x with a negative coefficient, resulting in a downward facing parabolic shape. The constant term $\frac{1}{\sqrt{2\pi\sigma^2}}$ in front of the exponential function serves as a normalization factor to ensure that the total area under the curve is 1 [74].

In Equation 3.2, similar to UVND, the argument of the exponential term is also in quadratic form, depending on the vector variable $\mathbf{x}$. For a single variable, the term $\frac{1}{2}(\mathbf{x} - \mu)^T \Sigma^{-1}(\mathbf{x} - \mu)$ simplifies to $\frac{(x-\mu)}{\sigma}$ to represent the number of standard deviations away from the mean. Similar to UVND, the term $\frac{1}{\sqrt{(2\pi)^p |\Sigma|}}$ is the normalization factor and the argument of the exponential term $-\frac{1}{2}(\mathbf{x} - \mu)^T \Sigma^{-1}(\mathbf{x} - \mu)$ is a downward facing quadratic bowl [74]. This quadratic term is called squared Mahalanobis distance (MD) which is the distance between the random vector $\mathbf{x}$ and the mean vector μ in multivariate space.

Using the PDF, the cumulative distribution function (CDF) of UVND for observation x can be obtained as,

$$
\begin{aligned}
F(x) &= \int_{-\infty}^{x} f(t; \mu, \sigma^2)\, dt \\
&= \frac{1}{\sqrt{2\pi\sigma^2}} \int_{-\infty}^{x} \exp\{-\frac{1}{2\sigma^2}(t - \mu)^2\}\, dt
\end{aligned}
\tag{3.3}
$$

Similarly, the CDF of MVND for observation vector $\mathbf{x}$ with p variables can be defined as,

$$
\begin{aligned}
F(\mathbf{x}) &= \int_{-\infty}^{x_1} \int_{-\infty}^{x_2} \cdots \int_{-\infty}^{x_p} f(t; \mu, \Sigma)\, dt_1\, dt_2 \ldots dt_p \\
&= \frac{1}{\sqrt{(2\pi)^p |\Sigma|}} \int_{-\infty}^{x_1} \int_{-\infty}^{x_2} \cdots \int_{-\infty}^{x_p} \\
&\quad \exp\{-\frac{1}{2}(\mathbf{t} - \mu)^T \Sigma^{-1}(\mathbf{t} - \mu)\}\, dt_1\, dt_2 \ldots dt_p
\end{aligned}
\tag{3.4}
$$

The concept of the Mahalanobis distance was first introduced by Indian statistician P.C. Mahalanobis in 1936 [75]. The MD is a widely used metric in multivariate statistics and has numerous applications across a range of fields. These include identifying outliers, classification, clustering, discriminant analysis, pattern recognition, principal component analysis, and others (e.g [76, 77]).

In this work we use MD based metric to sample data received from the vehicles. Each RSI in a region selects the observations which have lower MD and forwards it to a central server. The sampling factor for each RSI varies to meet the estimated network delay to reach the server. In multivariate space, the observations with lower MD are highly useful to be used for the classification tasks. These are the valueable observations which are highly useful to enable a ML model to better learn a decision boundary in multivariate space. The observations with higher MD are usually considered as outliers and that could mislead the ML models during learning.

Correlation matrix in Equation 3.2 is defined with the covariances between variables defined using correlation coefficient and standard deviations. For any two random variables X and Y, covariance $COV(X, Y)$ is defined as: correlation coefficient ρ_{xy} can be defined as:

$$
COV(X, Y) = \rho_{xy}\sigma_x\sigma_y
\tag{3.5}
$$

Where, σ_x and σ_y are the standard deviations of variables X and Y respectively and ρ_{xy} is the correlation coefficient between X and Y.

The concepts discussed in this section are used to generate synthetic dataset and calculate MD for each observation of the synthetic and real dataset.

3.4 Communication Efficient Centralized Learning for IoV: Proposed Approach

This section first presents the proposed system model followed by the proposed approach to achieve communication efficient centralized learning for IoV network. Figure 3.1 depicts the proposed system model, which highlights that smart vehicles are equipped with wireless communication technology that enables them to exchange important safety and other messages with nearby road-side infrastructure (RSI) and other vehicles. This facilitates safe navigation and access to a wide range of services.

In the proposed work, we consider service provider leverages ML activities centrally to utilize the tremendous volume of data generated in smart vehicles to constantly creating new services(s) and/or improving the existing services to create highly safe and enhanced IoV network. We assume that RSIs are installed alongside the road and that each RSI handles data exchange for a particular region. In the proposed learning framework, smart vehicles send their sensor data to a nearby RSI, and the RSI forwards the received data to a central server. The central server collects all such data from distributed RSIs and performs machine learning (ML) tasks with the acquired data.

In this scenario, forwarding all data received from vehicles by each RSI to the central server may cause communication issues that could hinder the efficient implementation of centralized learning for several reasons. One such reason could be high vehicular density, where the limited bandwidth of the transmission medium between an RSI and the central server must be shared among a larger number of vehicles. Another factor that can affect data transmission time is network traffic. If network traffic is high, the transmission of data to the server takes longer, and the communication link speed is also a key factor.

Given these challenges, the proposed approach employs a sampling strategy, whereby each

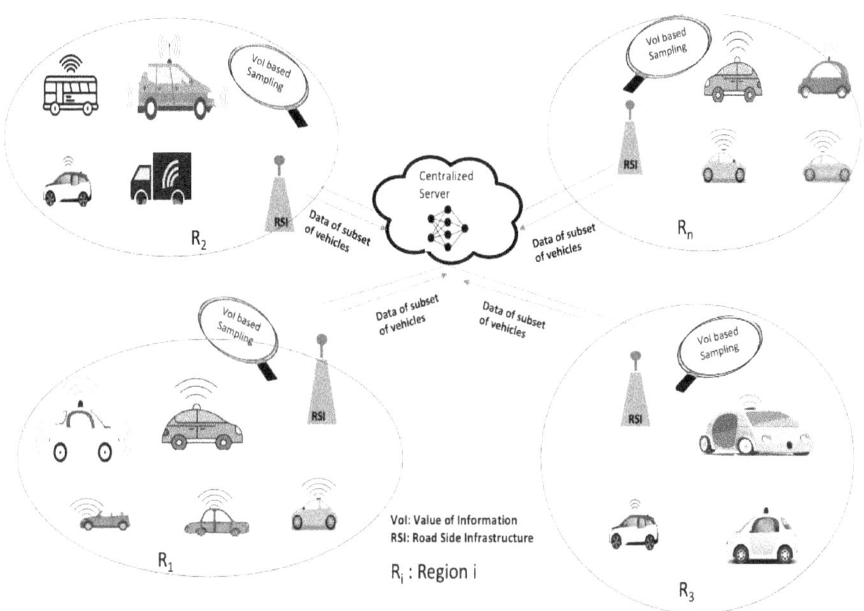

Figure 3.1. System Model for Communication Efficient Collaborative Learning for IoV

RSI forwards only a subset of the received data instead of all of it. However, in machine learning tasks, a larger number of training data is often required to improve model learning. This means that the sampling strategy could result in a loss of learning performance. To overcome this, the proposed approach uses a value-of-information-based sampling strategy. The underlying assumption behind this approach is that the data captured by vehicles may vary in quality from one vehicle to another due to factors such as noise, type and quality of resources, and other factors. Therefore, excluding vehicles that do not contribute useful information may not significantly affect learning performance, but it offers significant potential to reduce network traffic and improve the efficiency of centralized learning communication.

In this regard, in each region, a RSI selects a subset of vehicles with the higher VoI where the number of vehicles in a subset is decided as per the estimated network delay to reach a centralized server. In the paper, the term subset of vehicles is used interchangeably to mean subset of data from vehicles. Each RSI assess the value of information of received data using MD metric. The lower the MD of an observation, the higher the VoI it contains. The underlying assumption for

VoI is that for MVND, significant poportion of observations are centered around the mean of the MVND.

To achieve this, for each region, the RSI chooses a subset of vehicles with a higher Value of Information (VoI), where the size of the subset is determined based on the estimated network delay to the centralized server. In the paper, the term "subset of vehicles" is used interchangeably with "subset of data from vehicles." Each RSI evaluates the VoI of the received data using the MD metric, where a lower MD of an observation indicates a higher VoI. The underlying assumption for the VoI is that, for MVND, a significant proportion of useful observations are concentrated around the mean of the MVND.

The multitude of sensors equipped in vehicles provide valuable data to draw various inferences. The implementation of a machine learning approach that utilizes this sensor data to make predictions or classifications can greatly contribute to the safety, security, and efficiency of the IoV. To enable ML tasks, in each communication round initiated by a centralized server, a RSI in every region collects sensor data from N distinct vehicles within that region. Assuming that there are R geographical regions, we can label them as $r = 1, 2, \ldots, R$, and in each region, there exists a RSI denoted as $\mathcal{R}^r$. The proposed working scenario can be summarized as follows: a centralized server creates a machine learning model to represent a specific IoV service. To efficiently collect data for training and testing the model, the server initiates a communication round and sets a time budget within which it expects to receive data for that particular communication round.

Let c denote a communication round initiated by a server. The value of c starts from 1 when a service provider first creates a new ML-based service and it increases until the provider determines that the ML model does not require further updates.

Let, τ_c represents the time budget for round c. τ could be synchronized clock time by which server should receive the data belong to round c. At the beginning of each communication round c, the server broadcasts c and τ_c to all RSIs identified as region $\mathcal{R}^r$. Then, each $\mathcal{R}^r$ broadcasts a request to send data to vehicles in its region. Let, V_c^r represents the set of vehicles in a region r at communication round c and $|V_c^r|$ represents its cardinality. After receiving data from vehicles, each

$\mathcal{R}^r$ samples received data so as to meet the time constraint τ_c. Each $\mathcal{R}^r$ estimates the appropriate number of subset of vehicles considering the vehicular density in region r and estimating the network delay to reach the server. Delays in network are typically consists of processing delay, queuing delay, transmission delay and propagation delay. The network delay primarily determines the time to reach the vehicles' data from a RSI to the central server. However, the scope of this work is not to estimate the delay instead, this work presents a novel approach to create an efficient centralized learning environment by sampling valuable data which could demonstrate as close to if not better performance compared to the case of considering all the data. Extensive research has been conducted on the topic of network delay estimation, and we recommend that readers refer existing literature such as [78–81].

Sampling data to meet network quality and adjust to changing network scenarios presents a significant opportunity to establish a communication-efficient learning environment for the IoV.

3.5 Dataset Preparation and Simulation Setup

Initially, this section presents the preparation of the dataset, followed by the simulation setup designed to evaluate the performance of the proposed approach (in Section 5.5). The effectiveness of the proposed approach is tested on two datasets. The first dataset is generated synthetically, based on idealistic assumptions, where the random variables conform to a true normal distribution, and there is correlation among the random variables. The second dataset used is a real dataset obtained from the Kaggle site [82], which consists of On Board Diagnostics (OBD) Data collected from the Power Train Control Module of 14 drivers while they were driving their cars on their daily routes.

The purpose of evaluating the proposed approach on the synthetic dataset is to assess its performance in an ideal MVND scenario, while testing it on the actual dataset is intended to confirm its effectiveness in a real-world setting.

3.5.1 <u>Dataset Preparation</u>

Here, we first outline the preparation of the synthetic dataset, followed by the preparation of the real dataset.

Synthetic Dataset Preparation

To generate the synthetic dataset, we identified three crucial features that could be utilized to predict whether a vehicle is in a **safe** or **unsafe** condition. Categorizing a vehicle as unsafe indicates that it may unexpectedly malfunction while driving, which could pose a significant safety risk on the road. Therefore, if a vehicle can automatically identify the status of nearby vehicles, it can take the appropriate corrective measures to enhance safety. The three features we selected are the number of miles driven by a vehicle, the number of years it has been in operation, and its emission level. We designated these features as Miles, Years, and Emission, respectively. We set the mean vector for Miles, Years, and Emission as [100000, 15, 5] and the standard deviation as [25000, 3, 1], correspondingly. The correlation coefficients between variables were defined as $\rho_{Miles,Years} = 0.5$, $\rho_{Miles,Emission} = 0.8$, and $\rho_{Years,Emission} = 0.4$. These values are assigned under the assumption that a higher number of years of use does not necessarily equate to higher miles driven and emission levels. Nonetheless, as a vehicle is driven for more miles, the emission level is likely to increase. We used the "multivariate_normal" function under the "Scipy.stats" library in Python to produce a multivariate normal distribution. Subsequently, we generated a dataset consisting of 20,000 samples that adhere to that distribution.

In order to assign a class label of "safe" or "unsafe" to each observation, we made an assumption that if the number of miles driven, the number of years in operation, or the emission level of a vehicle is high or a combination of these variables is high, the vehicle is more likely to experience a malfunction. To make a reasonable approximation, we computed the cumulative distribution function value for each instance of the multivariate observation. We regarded the CDF value for the mean vector as a reference point, and all observations with a CDF greater than that for the mean vector were designated as "unsafe," while the remaining observations were considered "safe". The CDF was computed by utilizing the "cdf" function from the Python library "scipy.stats.multivariate_normal". The 3-dimensional scatter plot for each observation of the synthetic dataset with its corresponding class label is depicted in Figure 3.2.

Figures 3.5a, 3.5b, and 3.5c display the probability density function (PDF) plots for the distribution of each feature. Meanwhile, Figure 3.2 illustrates the 3-dimensional scatter plot for each observation alongside its corresponding class labels. Additionally, Figures 3.5a, 3.5b, and 3.5c also compare the distribution of the training samples (which will be discussed in 3.5.2) with that of all samples.

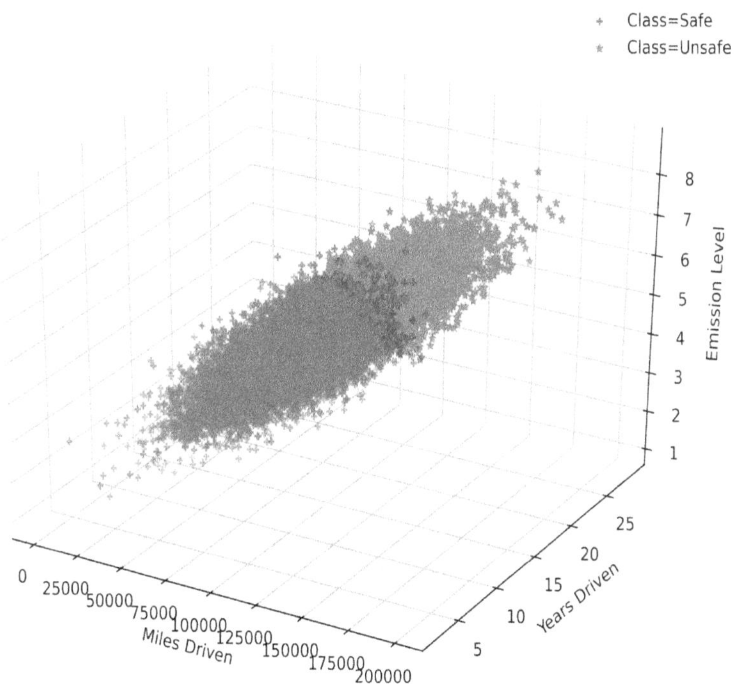

Figure 3.2. 3-D Scatter Plot for All Observations of Synthetic Dataset

Real Dataset Preparation

The real dataset downloaded from [82] consisted of 32 features, with a class label 'TROUBLE_-CODES'. The original shape of the dataset was (60439, 33), however, only 11925 instances had a 'TROUBLE_CODES' value provided. As part of the preprocessing, we removed all records where 'TROUBLE_CODES' were null and also deleted 13 columns containing more than 45% null values. Additionally, we removed two columns ('YEAR' and 'ENGINE_POWER') as they had the same single value. The dataset was mainly dominated by the two types of 'TROUBLE_-CODES', 'P0133' and 'C0300', which accounted for approximately 99% of the total data. We removed records containing other 'TROUBLE_CODES' that started with 'P0' to keep the the two main types of 'TROUBLE_CODES' and present the problem as binary classification.

In the following preprocessing step, we focused on the main objective of the dataset, which is generating a code based on observational values. Therefore, we kept only the columns related to the on board diagnostics observational values and deleted the remaining ones which included ['CAR_YEAR', 'DTC_NUMBER', 'VEHICLE_ID', 'MARK', 'TIMESTAMP', 'MODEL', 'AU-TOMATIC', 'MIN', 'HOURS', 'DAYS_OF_WEEK', 'MONTHS']. The 'DTC_NUMBER' column did not add additional meaning as it contained 'MIL is OFF1 codes' where 'TROUBLE_-CODES' was 'P0133' and 'MIL is OFF0 codes' where 'TROUBLE_CODES' was 'C0300'. We also deleted records where 50% or more of the columns were not filled. For the remaining columns that still contained null values, we replaced these with the mean value of the respective column. After this preprocessing, the dataset shape changed from (11925, 33) (considering only not-null 'TROUBLE_CODES') to (11740, 9). The histogram plot and correlation graph for the columns are shown in Figures 3.3 and 3.4, respectively.

3.5.2 Simulation Setup

The main aim of the simulation is to compare the ML performance of two scenarios - one where all the training data is considered and the other where only a sampled subset of the data is used, with the MD metric. Throughout the paper, the former scenario is referred to as the "standard approach," while the latter is referred to as the "proposed approach." Initially, both the real and synthetic datasets are randomly shuffled and split into an 80:20 proportion. The 20% of the dataset is used as the test set for both scenarios to compare their ML performance under the same validation

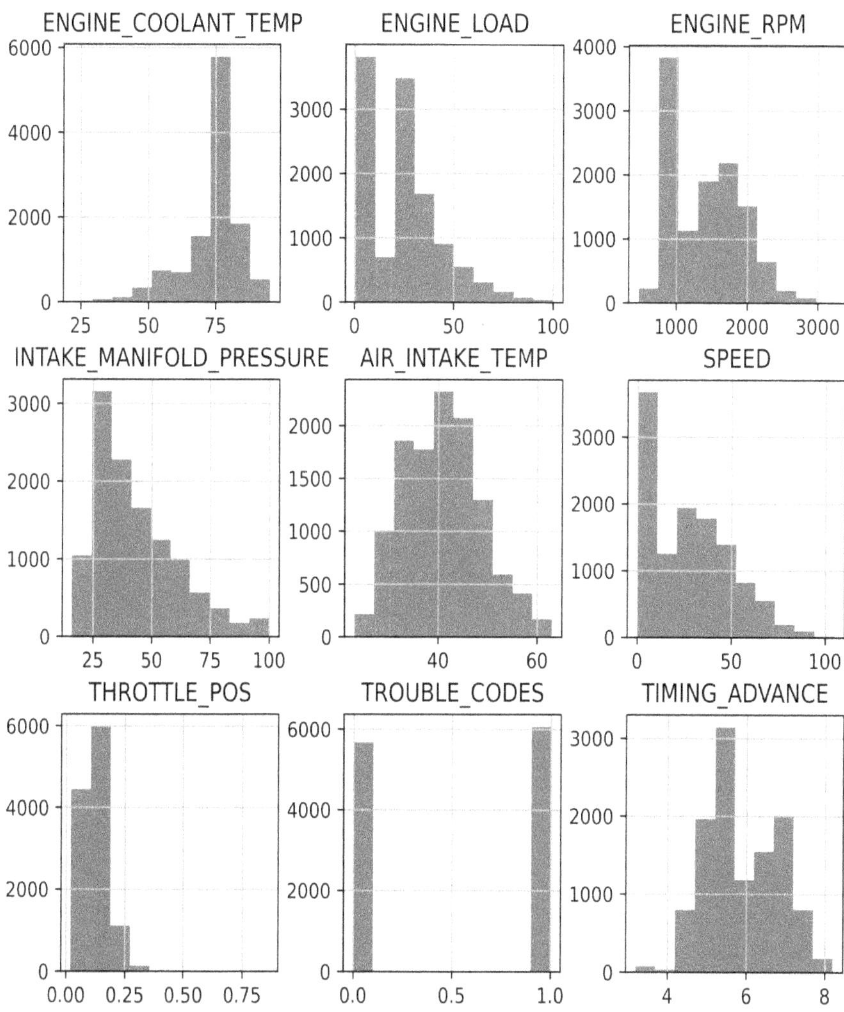

Figure 3.3. The Histogram Plot for each feature and class label (TROUBLE_CODES)

set. The remaining proportion, which contains 80% of the total dataset, is labeled as the D dataset with $|D|$ number of records. In the standard approach, D is used as the training set, while in the proposed approach, a sampled subset is created from D and used for training.

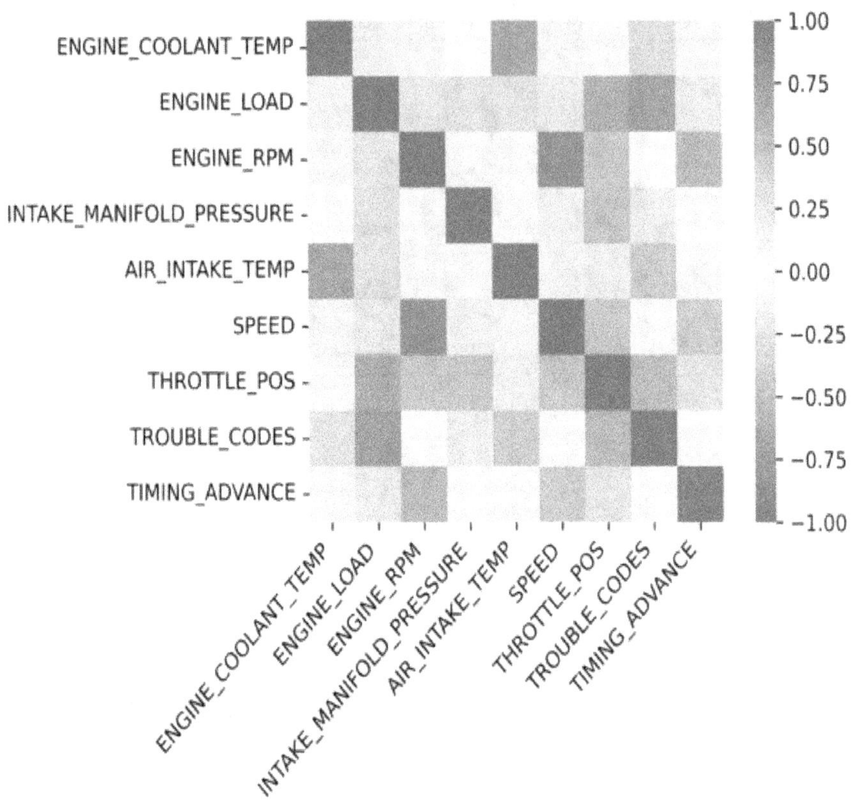

Figure 3.4. The Graphical Representation of the Correlation Matrix

Sampling Strategy for Synthetic Dataset

To implement the sampling strategy on dataset D, we began by randomly selecting the number of communication rounds C from the range of 5 to 10. We then divided D into C parts, denoted as D_c, each consisting of almost an equal number of records determined by floor division. Next, we randomly assigned a number of RSIs R from the range of 5 to 10. For each communication round $c = 1$ to C, we divided D_c into R parts, each consisting of almost an equal number of records. Then, for each $\mathcal{R}_r$ (r=1 to R), we calculated the MD for all of its samples and selected samples with lower MD values. To simulate network delay differences in different regions, in each communication round c, we randomly assigned a sampling percentage ranging from 10% to 90%

for each $\mathcal{R}_r$. Lower sampling percentages were used to mimic higher network delays, while higher values represented lower network delays. The sampled data from each $\mathcal{R}_r$ in each communication round c were collected to create a training set for the proposed approach.

A comparison between the probability density histograms of each feature of the sampled training data (52% of D set) and that of the all data is presented in Figure 3.5. Figures 3.5a, 3.5b, and 3.5c demonstrate that MD-based sampling selects observations that are more centered around the mean of the distribution.

Sampling Strategy for Real Dataset

The sampling strategy for the real dataset follows a similar approach as the one presented in 3.5.2. However, the distribution of the real dataset is not ideal and does not follow a normal distribution as the synthetic data. To address this, and to test the efficacy of the proposed approach in a real scenario, we tested the proposed approach on varying proportions of sampled training data. We ran the simulation for three iterations, and in each iteration, we assigned a sampling proportion to create training data with lower proportions. For the first iteration, the sampling proportion in a communication round c for each RSI R_r was set to a random value between 50% to 90%. In the following iterations, we reduced both the lower and upper sampling ranges by 20, resulting in sampling proportion ranges of 30% to 70% and 10% to 50% for the second and third iterations, respectively. In each iteration, each RSI used the MD metric to sample observations as per its respective sampling factor.

To present the true efficacy of the proposed approach in a real scenario, we also compared the performance of the proposed sampling strategy with a random sampling strategy. For the random sampling strategy, the training data was created in the same manner as the proposed sampling strategy, except that for the same sampling factor, each RSI sampled data randomly. Finally, for the real dataset, we compared the ML performance between the standard approach, the proposed approach, and the random approach.

The performance results for all these approaches will be presented and evaluated in the next

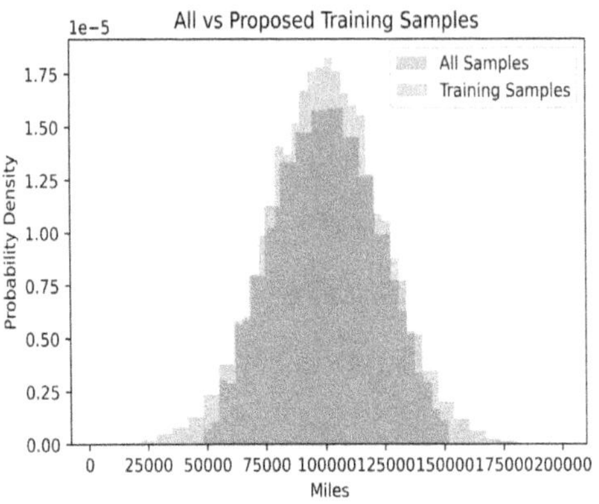

(a) PDF Plot for Miles Driven

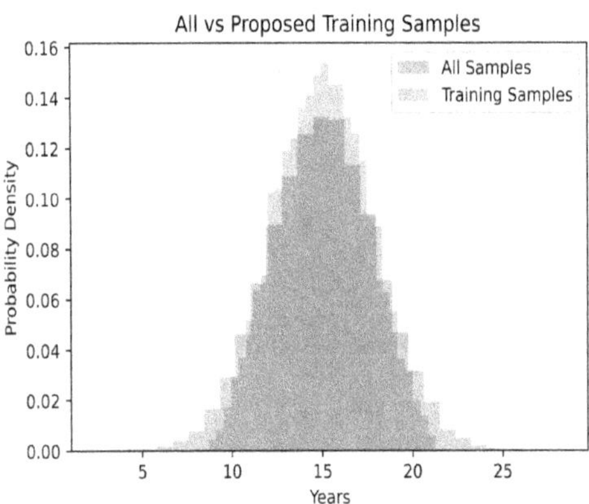

(b) PDF Plot for Operated Years

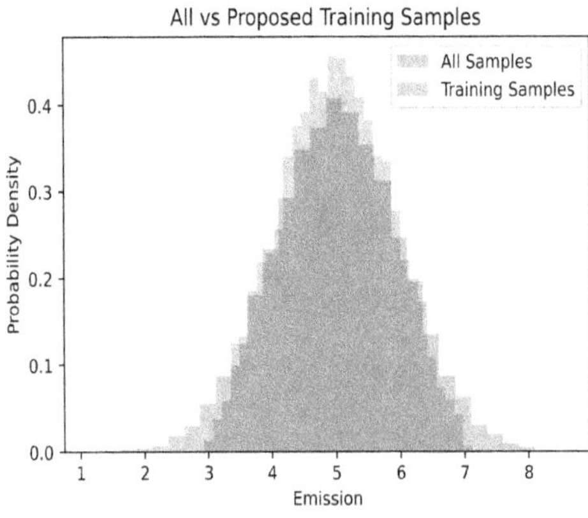

(c) PDF Plot for Emission Level

Figure 3.5. Probability Density Histogram of Features (All vs Sampled Training Data) for Synthetic Dataset

Section.

3.6 Performance Evaluation

In this section, the performance of the proposed approach is presented and compared with other approaches. Initially, we evaluate the ML performance on synthetic data, and then proceed to assess it on a real data.

Performance Evaluation on Synthetic Dataset

Given the nature of the data, we presumed that the support vector classifier (SVC) would be an appropriate choice. Nonetheless, we also evaluated the performance by considering a deep learning neural network (DNN) for assessing the proposed approach. The training data for the proposed approach was created using a sampling technique discussed in Section 3.5.2. The DNN we examined consisted of a multilayer perceptron with 12 and 8 nodes in two hidden layers between the input and output layers, respectively. The loss function used was 'binary_crossentropy', and the optimizer used was 'admm' with a learning_rate of 0.001. Sigmoid activation was used for the output layer, while linear activation was used for the other layers. The results of the simulation for various performance metrics are shown in Figures 3.6 and 3.7.

Figure 3.6 shows the progression of training and validation loss, and Figure 3.7 shows the progression of training and validation accuracy for the DNN model for both the standard approach and the proposed approach over the 300 epochs.

The performance of the DNN model for the training data only is satisfactory. For the validation data, we can observe an overall upward trend for the validation accuracy and a downward trend in the validation loss, but there are frequent fluctuations over the epochs. One possible explanation for this is that the final output from the Sigmoid function fluctuates around 0.5, causing the loss to fluctuate as well. Consequently, a small change in the model parameters in each epoch can result in a large change in the final accuracy. Despite the loss seeming to approach zero, there are still fluctuations that may not be noticeable upon manual inspection due to scaling. However, the thick

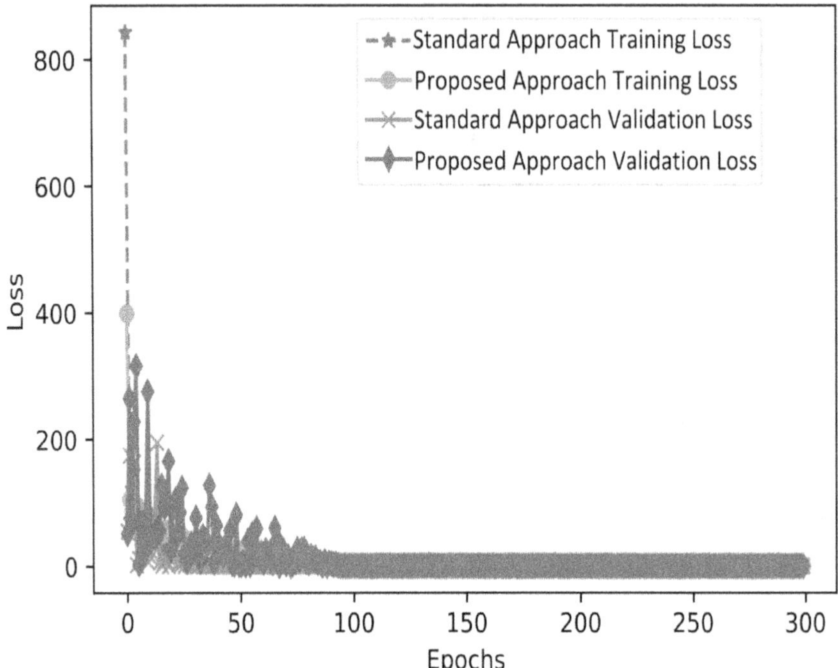

Figure 3.6. History of Training Loss and Validation Loss

line of the loss indicates that it does not have a consistent downward trend. The performance of

the DNN model for the sampled data (proposed approach) is even worse failing to generalize well

from the lower proportion of training data. The DNN model fails to learn the intrinsic distribution

of the data. This clearly indicated that the neural network is not suitable for this scenario.

Consequently, we trained and tested SVC on a synthetic dataset that was created using the

approach discussed in Section 3.5.1. The classifier was configured with the 'rbf' kernel. The

performance comparison between the standard approach and the proposed approach is illustrated

in Figure 3.8.

As shown in the precision-recall curve and the test accuracy depicted in Figure 3.8, SVC was

highly effective in discerning the hyperplane from the multivariate distribution of synthetic train-

ing data. Additionally, despite being trained on nearly half the dataset, the proposed approach

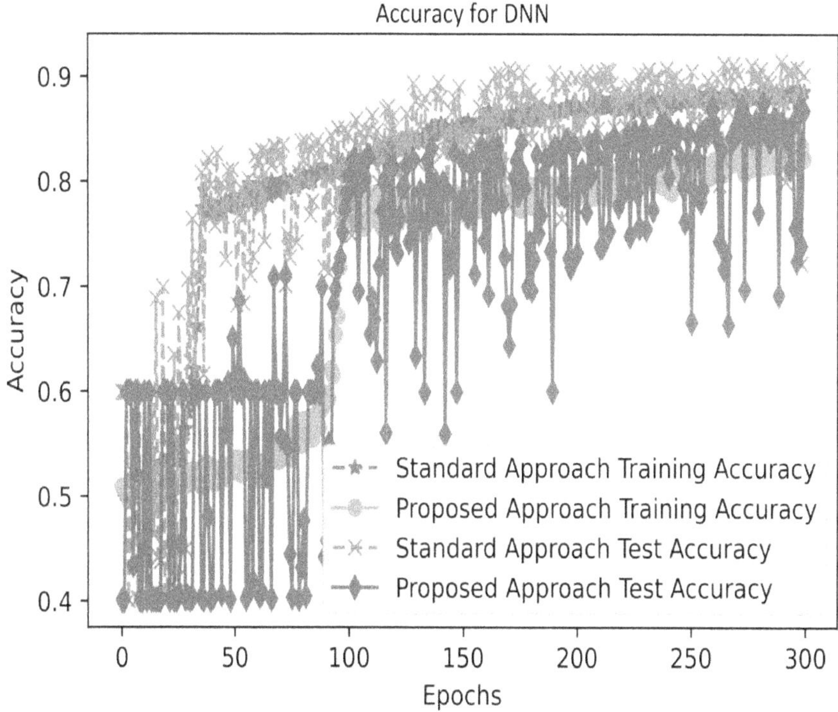

Figure 3.7. History of Training and Validation Accuracies

performed almost as well as the standard approach. This performance indicates that MD is a useful metric for data filtering, which can result in nearly identical performance compared to using all the available data.

The proposed approach performed effectively with SVC model to demonstrate the possibility to create a communication efficient IoV network without noticeable performance loss. Next, we confirm the effectiveness of the proposed approach testing it on real vehicular dataset.

3.6.1 Performance Evaluation on Real Dataset

To evaluate the performance of the proposed approach on real-world vehicular data, we employed the same SVC model that was used for the synthetic dataset. We obtained the processed real dataset, as described in Section 3.5.1, and created training datasets for different approaches using

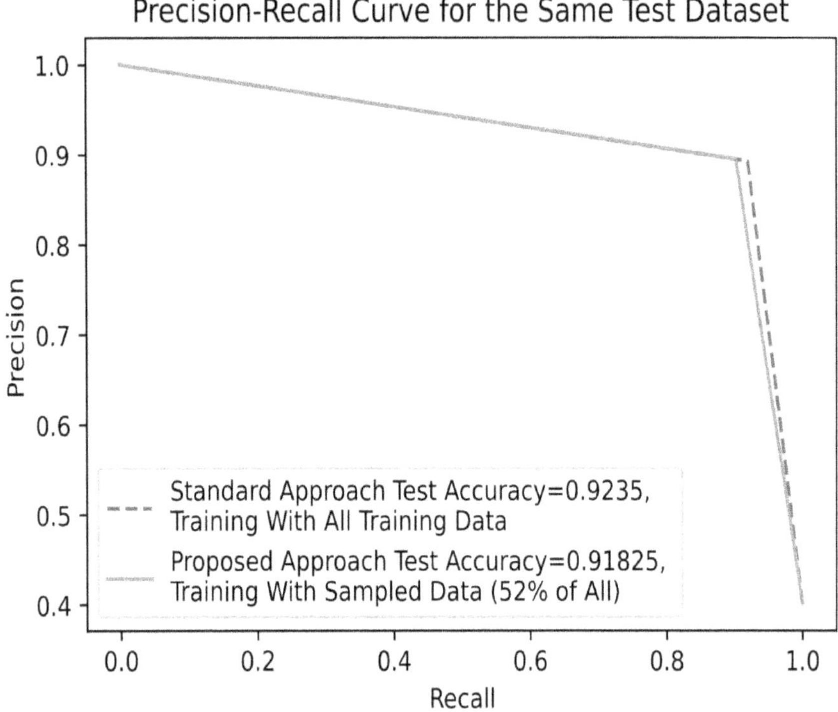

Figure 3.8. Precision Recall Curve (All Data Vs 52% Sampled Data)

the sampling techniques presented in Section 3.5.2. Figures 3.9 and 3.10 provide a comparison of the performance of all three approaches.

In Figure 3.9, we present a comparison of the training and test accuracy for the standard approach, proposed approach, and random approach. To evaluate performance, we measured the test accuracy of each approach using the same test dataset after training with different approaches for three iterations. Our results indicate that the proposed approach performed effectively achieving accuracy levels that were comparable to those of the standard approach despite the significant reduction in training data during successive iterations. In contrast, the training and testing accuracy of the random approach significantly decreased during the third iteration, where only about 30% of randomly sampled training data was used.

Figure 3.9 illustrates the performance comparison of the standard approach, proposed ap-

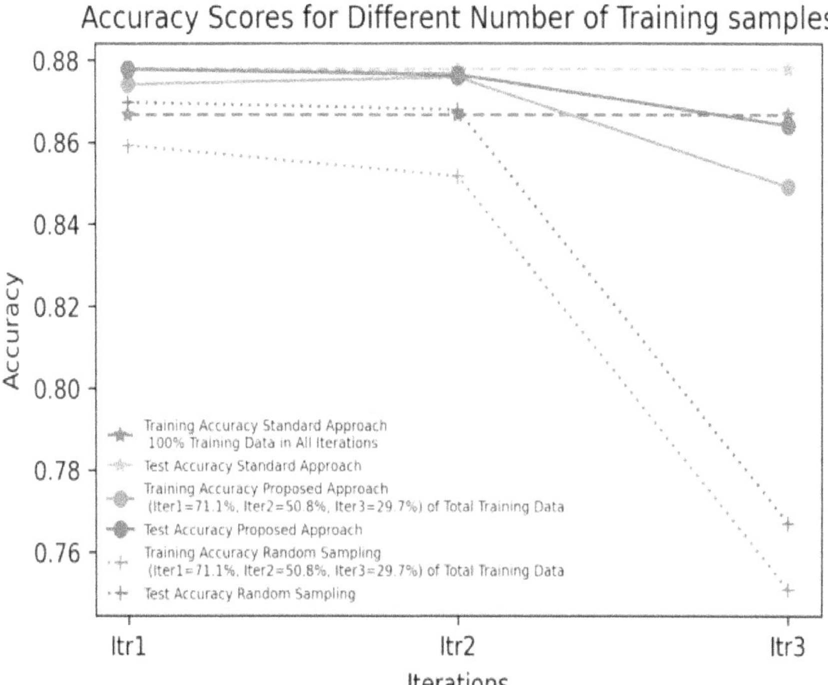

Figure 3.9. Accuracy Comparison for the Three Different Approaches.

proach, and random approach in terms of training and test accuracy. To evaluate performance, we measured the test accuracy of each approach on the same test dataset after training with different approaches for three iterations. Our results indicate that the proposed approach performed effectively to demonstrate similar performance to the standard approach despite the significant reduction in training data during successive iterations. Conversely, the training and testing accuracy of the random approach decreased significantly during the third iteration, where only about 30% of randomly sampled training data was used.

Figure 3.10 displays a detailed analysis of the classifier's performance in terms of the confusion matrix. The standard approach (Figure 3.10a) shows that the classifier tends to misclassify code2 examples as code1, resulting in slightly higher false negative predictions. The proposed approach (Figure 3.10b) demonstrates balanced performance up to two iterations. However, in the third iteration, where only about 30% of the sampled training data was used, the model tended to

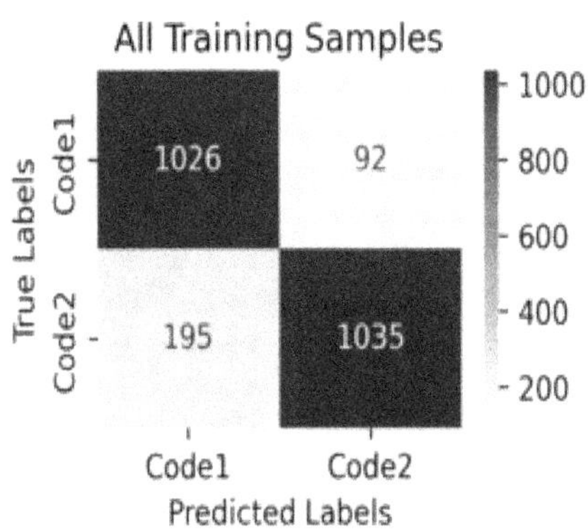

(a) Confusion Matrix for Standard Approach

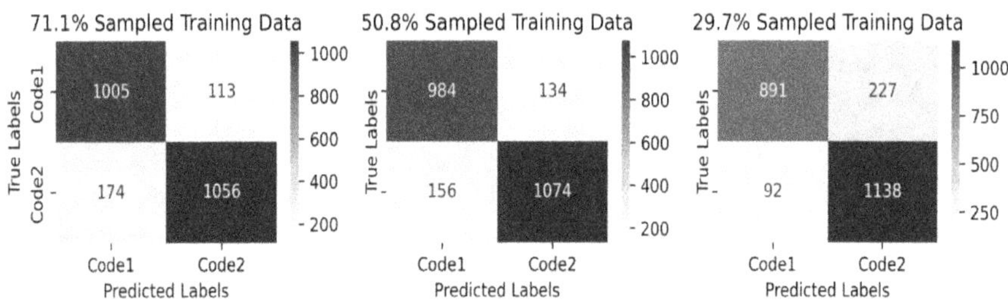

(b) Confusion Matrix for Proposed Approach

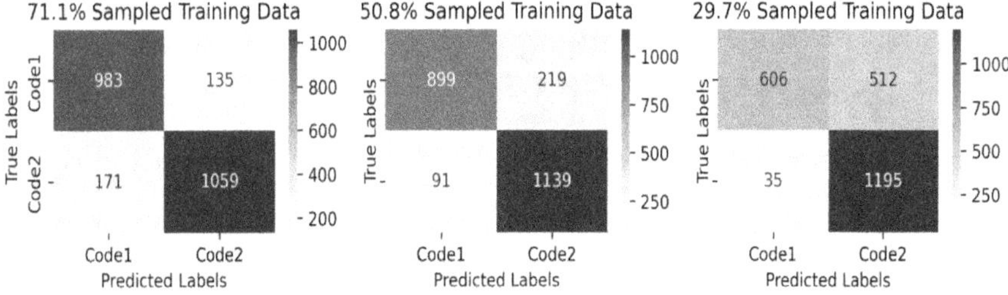

(c) Confusion Matrix for Random Sampling Approach

Figure 3.10. Confusion Matrix on the same Test Dataset for all approaches.

misclassify code1 as code2, resulting in slightly higher false positive predictions. In contrast, for the random approach (Figure 3.10c), the classifier failed to detect code1 correctly from the second iteration, and the false positive predictions increased significantly in the third iteration, where only about 30% of the randomly sampled data was used for training.

The results of the performance comparison indicate that the proposed method of sampling data by leveraging the MD metric to exploit multivariate normal distribution was highly effective for both synthetic and real datasets. Even when up to 50% of the total training data for synthetic datasets was sampled, the proposed approach demonstrated almost identical results to the standard approach. Similarly, for the real dataset, the proposed approach was satisfactory even with just 30% of the available training data being sampled. These findings validate the potential of the proposed approach in establishing an efficient centralized learning network for IoV.

3.7 Chapter Summary

In order to address the communication challenge in distributed learning for IoV, this paper proposed a novel method of using the MD metric to sample vehicles' data. The effectiveness of this approach was tested on both synthetic and real datasets, comparing the machine learning performance of the sampled data with that of the complete dataset. The proposed approach was further examined through different sampling ratios and alternative strategies. The proposed method demonstrated significant efficacy by producing outcomes comparable to using the entire dataset with only approximately 50% of the sampled data. Even with a smaller sample size of just 30% of the total, the approach generated satisfactory results, indicating its potential to establish a communication efficient distributed learning network for the Internet of Vehicles (IoV).

CHAPTER 4.   ANOMALY DETECTION IN FEDERATED LEARNING FOR INTERNET OF VEHICLES

4.1 Introduction

Machine Learning (ML) is on the verge of transitioning from centralized, distributed to federated learning (FL) due to the inherent privacy-preserving framework by FL. Vehicles in IoV are directly connected to the private information of the drivers/owners, so FL could help to provide a great deal of privacy while using ML models. FL enables collaborative learning among participants just by exchanging updated model parameters with the FL server while keeping training data local in the end devices which is suitable for vehicular communications. However, this learning framework makes the life of the server difficult to detect the malicious behavior of participants. Malicious model updates from participants may affect the accuracy of the learning model considerably and consequently may cause severe consequences in the Internet of Vehicles (IoV) environment.

To address this issue, this chapter investigates a novel approach to apply Shiryaev's quickest change detection (QCD) [15] technique in the FL realm. QCD is applied to detect abnormal changes in statistical properties of model parameters in FL as quickly as possible. We apply QCD on the server-side in two ways. First, QCD is applied to detect a change in the statistical properties over the model parameters sent by the participating devices. Second, QCD is applied to the history of aggregated model parameters. The first approach facilitates identifying malicious clients which can be eliminated in future learning activities. The other approach assists the server to roll back to an earlier version of the model in case of identifying the anomaly in the aggregated parameters value. As QCD is applied on the server-side, it does not add any computation overhead on the client-side as well as communication overheard during transmission. These two approaches are evaluated with the help of numerical results.

The remainder of this chapter is organized as follows. Section 4.2 presents related work. Section 4.3 presents a system model. QCD and the proposed approach is presented in Section 4.4. Numerical results are included in Section 4.5. Finally, Section 4.6 concludes the chapter.

4.2 Related Work

Sequential analysis is one of the most powerful data analysis tools in many fields including finance, science, engineering, and others. Quickest Change Detection (QCD), a sub-class of sequential analysis, has got significant research interest since its earliest works (e.g.[16], [83]). Since then, it has been applied to a wide range of applications belong to a broad spectrum of fields such as network intrusion detection ([e.g.[84]), anomaly detection (e.g.[85]), multi-sensor systems (e.g.[86–88]), detecting biological problems (e.g. [89]), monitoring cracks and damages to vital bridges and highway networks [90], quickest short-term voltage instability detection in power systems [91], quickest spectrum sensing in cognitive radio [92], failure detection in manufacturing systems and many more. Among several use cases, some works (e.g.[86–88]) detect abnormal change in statistical properties of the data observed from distributed sensors. A typical setting of a multi-sensor environment is, a centralized fusion center collects messages from distributed sensors and makes a decision when it detects changes. Although QCD has been applied in a wide range of fields, it has not yet been applied in FL where sensors' data is kept local and only learned model parameters are sent to a centralized server. To the best of our knowledge, this is the first work in FL scenario aiming to detect an abnormal change in a statistical property of exchanged parameters from distributed participants.

The FL framework inherently supports privacy and security however, concerns such as poisoning and reverse-engineering attacks have been pointed out in literature in recent times [7, 8, 93]. To address these threats, techniques like differential privacy (e.g. [94]), secure multi-party computation (SMC) (e.g. [95]), homographic encryption (HE) (e.g. [96]) have been proposed and tested by researchers. However, these techniques not only add extra computation and communication burden but also are not useful when client itself is malicious. FL has leveraged ML tasks to the end devices and it has widened the attack surface. In any network, detecting an abnormal behavior of a client is always a difficult problem. It is even more difficult in the case of FL since only the model parameters are sent to the server. The accuracy of a global model solely depends on the model parameters sent by the clients. If the data or model parameters of clients are forged, it correspondingly affects the accuracy of the global model. Detecting the abnormal behavior of clients in FL is still an open research topic and needs to be addressed for the true applicability of FL. However, to address client-side anomaly, Fung et al. [97] presented an FL model FoolsGold that identifies Sybil attack based on the diversity of client updates in a distributed learning process. Byzantine-tolerant learning in distributed setting has been addressed in some works [98–100] but, most of them assume participant's data is unmodified and equally distributed. However, none of these works analyze individual client's behavior which is quite critical in IoV scenario. In this paper, we analyze individual client's behavior and detect anomalies in the exchanged parameters by applying QCD in the FL scenario for IoV. QCD is quick enough to detect a change in statistical properties of parameters without adding any computational burden (in the client-side) and communication overhead since we apply QCD solely on the server-side.

4.3 System Model

In this section, we present the system model for IoV where vehicles use FL, as shown in Fig. 4.1. The system model consists of server (mobile drone or road side edge server) and heterogeneous vehicles such as cars and trucks equipped with various smart sensors and dedicated short-range communication (DSRC) technology (such as the IEEE 802.11p standard devices) which enables sharing and exchanging of information wirelessly among vehicles using vehicle-to-vehicle (V2V) and vehicle-to-infrastructure (V2I) communications [101]. Vehicles are expected to exchange basic safety messages periodically as well as other information such as collision warning, lane changeing information, emergency warning, up-to-date traffic information, active navigation, infotainment, and so on. Cellular infrastructures and roadside units (RSU) are placed beside the roads to provide safety and other roadside services to vehicles.

When a service provider (SP) feels to improve the quality and/or the user experience of an

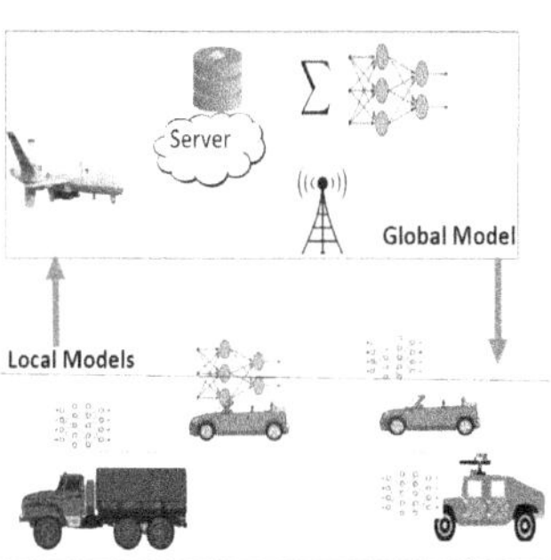

Figure 4.1. System Model with Federated Learning where local learning models/parameters are offloaded to the server and global model is broadcast back.

offered application, FL starts with creating a corresponding learning task. A general or pre-trained model is then distributed to the vehicles and the participating vehicles personalize the model locally with its local raw data. Vehicles perform ML tasks locally and send their parameters to the server. The server then aggregates all the updates received from the clients and performs ML tasks and finally distributes the updated model to the clients [6]. This is a continuous process by which the vehicles are constantly provided with all the new and emerging global knowledge.

4.4 Quickest Change Detection (QCD) and Proposed Approach

4.4.1 Quickest Change Detection (QCD)

QCD also known as quickest change-point detection or quickest detection is a technique used to detect an abrupt change in statistical properties of a stochastic system with a minimal detection delay. QCD analyzes the probability distribution of observations of a stochastic process and aims to detect an abrupt change in the distribution as quickly as possible minimizing false alarm. The earliest works on QCD [16, 83] are attributed to Shewhart for quality control by detecting a change in the manufacturing process. In a basic QCD problem, a stochastic observational model is represented by a sequence of random variables $\{X_n\}$, where $n = 1, 2, ...$, which are independent and identically distributed (i.i.d) with some probability density function (pdf). It is assumed that the distributions of $\{X_n\}$ change at some unknown time t from some pdf $f_0(x)$ to pdf $f_1(x)$. Pdfs f_0 and f_1 are called pre-change and post-change distributions and that is completely known to the observer. With the given sequential observations of $\{X_n\}$, the main goal of QCD is to detect t as quickly as possible. In literature, QCD has been extensively studied in Bayesian and non-Bayesian settings.

This dissertation considers Shiryaev's formulation for identifying an abrupt change in the distribution of parameters sent by the vehicles that participated in FL. Shiryaev's technique as formulated by Shriyaev [17, 18], gives optimal solution to minimize expected detection delay (EDD) subject to Probability of False Alarm (PFA) constraint. for i.i.d. model in Bayesian setting. In Shiryaev's formulation, the change point t is modeled as a random variable with a known geometric distribution. For our approach, we use Shiryaev's formulation for identifying an abrupt change in the distribution of parameters sent by the vehicles that participated in FL. There are other variations of QCD for the non-Bayesian setting and/or non-i.i.d model and we encourage readers to refer [15] for the details of these variations. In this paper, we only discuss QCD for i.i.d. model in Bayesian setting as formulated by Shriyaev [17, 18]. In a stochastic process, an observer sequentially takes observations for $\{X_n\}$. At each time slot n, an observer either stop and declare a change in the distribution or continue to take the next observation. The point of time at which the observer declares change and stop is called stop time represented by κ and the point at which distribution changes is called change point represented by Υ [15].

In the Bayesian setting, change point Υ is modeled with parameter ϱ. The probability that change point Υ occurs at n is specified as

$$\pi_n = \mathbb{P}\{\Upsilon = n\} = \varrho(1 - \varrho)^{n-1}\mathbb{I}_{\{n \geq 1\}}, \pi_0 = 0 \tag{4.1}$$

where $0 < \varrho < 1$ and $\mathbb{I}_{\{n \geq 1\}} = (1 - \pi_0)$ is an indicator function. The goal of QCD is to choose κ in the observation sequence $\{X_n\}$ to minimize expected detection delay (EDD) while satisfying constraint on probability of false alarm. The EDD and PFA are defined as follows.

$$EDD(\kappa) = \mathbb{E}[(\kappa - \Upsilon)^+] = \sum_{n=0}^{\infty} \pi_n \mathbb{E}_n[(\kappa - \Upsilon)^+] \tag{4.2}$$

$$PFA(\kappa) = \mathbb{P}(\kappa < \Upsilon) = \sum_{n=0}^{\infty} \pi_n \mathbb{P}_n(\kappa < \Upsilon) \tag{4.3}$$

Class of stopping time κ satisfying PFA is defined as:

$C_\alpha = \{\kappa : PFA(\kappa) \leq \alpha\}$, α is constraint on PFA. We now present Shiryaev's algorithm to find stopping time $\kappa \in C_\alpha$ to minimize EDD. Let us consider that $X_1^n = (X_1, X_2, ...X_n)$ represents observations up to time n. For for a given X_1^n, the posterior probability at time n that the change has taken place is defined as,

$$p_n = \mathbb{P}(\Upsilon \leq n | X_1^n) \tag{4.4}$$

p_n is also called Shiryaev-Robert (SR) statistic [17, 102] as its value is used to detect abrupt change in distribution. For next observations, p_{n+1} can be formulated recursively using Bayes' rule as,

$$p_{n+1} = \Phi(X_{n+1}, p_n) \tag{4.5}$$

with

$$\Phi(X_{n+1}, p_n) = \frac{\tilde{p}_n L(X_{n+1})}{\tilde{p}_n L(X_{n+1}) + (1 - p_n)} \tag{4.6}$$

where $\tilde{p}_n = p_n + (1 - p_n)\varrho$, $L(X_{n+1}) = \frac{f_1(X_{n+1})}{f_0(X_{n+1})}$ is the likelihood ratio, and $p_0 = 0$. The optimal solution to find stopping time as given by Shiryaev's algorithm is,

$$\kappa_s = \inf\{n \geq 1 : p_n \geq A_\alpha\} \tag{4.7}$$

where A_α is chosen such that $PFA(\kappa_s) = \alpha$. (For proof of (4.7), refer to [15]). We now also present alternate descriptions of Shiryaev's statistics and which are,

$$\wedge_n = \frac{p_n}{(1 - p_n)} \tag{4.8}$$

$$R_{n,\varrho} = \frac{p_n}{(1 - p_n)\varrho} \tag{4.9}$$

Where, for time slot n, $\wedge_n$ is the likelihood ratio of hypothesis "$H_1 : \Upsilon \leq n$" and "$H_0 : \Upsilon > n$" averaged over some change point $k \leq n$. For observations $X_1^n = (X_1, X_2, ... X_n)$

$$\begin{aligned}
\wedge_n &= \frac{\mathbb{P}(\Upsilon \leq n | X_1^n)}{\mathbb{P}(\Upsilon > n | X_1^n)} \\
&= \frac{\sum_{k=1}^{n}(1-\varrho)^{(k-1)}\varrho \prod_{i=1}^{k-1} f_0(X_i) \prod_{i=k}^{n} f_1(X_i)}{(1-\varrho)^n \prod_{i=1}^{n} f_0(X_i)} \\
&= \frac{1}{(1-\varrho)^n} \sum_{k=1}^{n}(1 - \varrho)^{(k-1)}\varrho \prod_{i=k}^{n} L(X_i)
\end{aligned} \tag{4.10}$$

where the likelihood ratio $L(X_i) = \frac{f_1(X_i)}{f_0(X_i)}$. Then we can write

$$\wedge_n = \frac{1}{(1 - \varrho)^n} \sum_{k=1}^{n}(1 - \varrho)^{(k-1)} \prod_{i=k}^{n} L(X_i) \tag{4.11}$$

In equation 4.9, $R_{n,\varrho}$ is just a scaled version of $\wedge_n$. Then, $R_{n,\varrho}$ for next observation can be computed recursively as,

$R_{n+1,\varrho} = \frac{1+R_{n,\varrho}}{1-\varrho} L(X_{n+1})$ where initially $R_{0,\varrho} = 0$.

For alternative descriptions of Shiryaev's statistics, corresponding Shiryaev stopping time expressions are as follows:

$$\kappa_s = \inf\{n \geq 1 : p_n \geq A\} \tag{4.12}$$

$$\kappa_s = \inf\{n \geq 1 : \wedge \geq a\} \tag{4.13}$$

$$\kappa_s = \inf\{n \geq 1 : R_{n,\varrho} \geq \frac{a}{\varrho}\} \tag{4.14}$$

where $a = \frac{A}{1-A}$.

4.4.2 QCD in Federated Learning for IoV

In the IoV scenario, there might be multiple learning tasks e.g. driving in different geographical scenarios, in different weather conditions, different traffic conditions, efficient routing, and so on. A server might select vehicles based on the suitability of learning tasks e.g. vehicles operating in snowing regions are selected for learning task of how to efficiently drive in snow condition. For simplicity, we formulate and simulate the proposed approach for one learning task which is similarly applicable to other learning tasks too. For the IoV, we assume that each learned task goes over series of convergences over time as per the changing need of improvement of the current model. So, a vehicle is likely to take part in the training of the different versions of the same learning task multiple times. We also assume that a vehicle is selected for reporting its parameters more often and the server needs to act promptly compared to other applications like FL for smartphones.

We now mathematically formulate expressions for the proposed approach to apply QCD on the exchanged parameters.

Let, V_n where $n = 1, 2...N$ are set of vehicles connected to the federated network. r where $r = 1, 2...$ represents different reporting rounds initiated by the server.

$A_{k,r}$ where $k = 1, 2...K$ are subset of N vehicles that are selected by the server for a particular reporting round r. For simplicity, we assume K vehicles report updates to the server.

Parameters w_l with $l = 1, 2...L$ are L different parameters of the learning model which are exchanged between vehicles and server. $w_{l,r}^k$ represents value of parameter w_l sent by A_k in r^{th} reporting round.

Aggregating server collect all such $w_{l,r}^k$ from K clients and aggregate the parameters. For each l and r, $\overline{W}_{l,r} = \sum_{k=1}^{K} \frac{n_k}{n} w_{l,r}^k$ is the weighted sum of parameters of link l of K vehicles in reporting round r. Where, n_k represents the number of local examples of $A_{k,r}$ and n represents total number of examples of current reporting round r.

We aim to detect an abrupt change in the distribution of exchanged parameters using QCD in two different ways. In the first way, when the server receives parameters from a participant, it checks the behavior of the participant using QCD.

It analyzes the history of parameters sent by the client including recent updated parameters. In the FL proposed in [6], the parameters of the clients are discarded after the aggregation however, considering the severity of operations for IoV, we assume it is worth to keep the history of exchanged parameters and analyze it to detect an anomaly. In the other way, the server analyzes the history of the aggregated parameters link by link using QCD. These two approaches of applying QCD are required as (i) if some participants act maliciously from the beginning, it might be hard to detect a change in such clients' behavior. So, applying QCD in aggregated parameters might detect such malicious behavior. (ii) If some clients coordinate to act maliciously and change parameters' value in such a way that aggregated parameters' value remains the same in subsequent rounds, then applying QCD in the first scenario is likely to detect malicious behavior of such clients. For example, if we consider the FL scenario for smartphones distributed around the world, for a specific learning task, data distribution is likely to be non-i.i.d. It is due to the wide scope of usages of smartphones such as usage based on age group, geographical location, heterogeneity of devices, and others. However, in IoV scenario, for a specific learning task, the usage of vehicles is restricted. The amount of local data collected may vary from vehicle to vehicle whereas the nature of data collected by vehicles is likely to be similar for a given scenario. For these reasons, we assume the distribution of parameters to be i.i.d. and apply Shiryaev's QCD algorithm which works optimally in the Bayesian setting.

We use SR statistic $R_{n,\varrho}$ as defined in (4.11) to find change in the distribution of parameters. We present a mathematical formulation for one vehicle for one particular link and similarly, it applies to other participants for others link. Let us consider that a vehicle has participated (including current participation) up to $r = 1, 2, ...x$ reporting rounds. Then, SR statistic for a link l and reporting round r can be written as

$$R_{x,\varrho} = \frac{1}{(1 - \varrho)^x} \sum_{r=1}^{x} (1 - \varrho)^{(r-1)} \prod_{i=r}^{x} L(W_{l,i}^k) \tag{4.15}$$

As defined in (4.6), the likelihood ratio $L(W_{l,i}^k) = \frac{f_1(W_{l,i}^k)}{f_0(W_{l,i}^k)}$. The value of reporting rounds initiated by the server is likely to be quite high compared to the rounds that each vehicle actually participates. It is so as it is not guaranteed that each vehicle is selected at every reporting rounds. However, when the participation of each vehicle is quite high which means when x is high, QCD can be applied efficiently using recursion by considering a time slot for reporting rounds. This case is shown in the second approach which can also be applied to the first approach in the same way. For the second approach, let total reporting rounds is partitioned in to time window of mth reporting rounds as $r = 1, 2, ...m, m + 1...2m, 2m + 1....$ To detect a change in the distribution of aggregated parameters in this setting, SR statistic is

$$R_{m,\varrho} = \frac{1}{(1 - \varrho)^m} \sum_{r=1}^{m} (1 - \varrho)^{(r-1)} \prod_{i=r}^{m} L(\overline{W}_{l,i}) \tag{4.16}$$

$R_{m,\varrho}$ of link l for next m rounds can be computed recursively as. $R_{m+1,\varrho} = \frac{1+R_{m,\varrho}}{1-\varrho} L(\overline{W}_{l,m+1})$ and $R_{0,\varrho} = 0$ initially As defined in (4.6), likelihood ratio $L(\overline{W}_{l,i}) = \frac{f_1(\overline{W}_{l,i})}{f_0(\overline{W}_{l,i})}$. Threshold to detect change in both cases is, $R_{th} = \frac{a}{\varrho}$ (as defined in Equation 4.14). The algorithmic steps for the first approach are summarized in Algorithm 1.

The algorithmic steps for the second approach are summarized in Algorithm 2.

In the next section, we simulate our proposed approach and discuss the results.

Algorithm 1: QCD with Shiryaev statistics for each client in FL

Result: Shiryaev statistics

for *Each client* **do**
    Receive learning parameters;
    Calculate $R_{x,\varrho}$;
    if $R_{x,\varrho} > R_{th}$ **then**
        Change detected, exclude such client(s) or its parameters from further learning activities;
    else
        No change detected, include these parameters;
    end
end

Algorithm 2: QCD with Shiryaev statistics for aggregated parameters in FL.

Result: Shiryaev statistics

for *Each reporting round* **do**
    Calculate aggregated value of parameters;
    Calculate $R_{m,\varrho}$;
    if $R_{m,\varrho} > R_{th}$ **then**
        Change detected, SP may select previous better model;
    else
        No change detected, continue same process in next reporting round;
    end
end

4.5 Performance Evaluation

For the performance evaluation of the proposed approach presented above, we performed simulations in two scenarios. In the first scenario (to detect malicious clients from reported parameters), among many participants/vehicles in federated learning, we considered a few out of these (say 10 vehicles) to analyze its reported parameters using QCD. Out of those, we selected a number of malicious clients randomly from 1% to a maximum of 50%. We assigned a number of reporting rounds that clients have participated (including current) to a random value from 200 to 300. While sending parameters to the server, if the client is malicious, it sends weight parameters with some perturbation.

The learning weights are generated following uniform distribution with mean 0 for genuine clients but with randomly perturbed mean from 0 to 0.3 for malicious clients. The generated parameters are reported to the server where Shiryaev's algorithm is applied to detect a change in distribution as quickly as possible. For the experiment, we assigned $\varrho = 0.01$, $A = 0.99$ and use SR statistic $R_{x,\varrho}$ and apply Shiryaev's detection. The results for the first scenario is presented in Fig. 4.2.

As shown in Fig. 4.2, a change is detected and the process is stopped when $R_{x,\varrho}$ crosses the threshold, otherwise the algorithm continuously calculates $R_{x,\varrho}$ for all observations. As we can see in the Fig. 4.2, there are malicious clients which have weight distribution with perturbed mean with values 0.183 and 0.206, respectively. For mean value 0.183, change point is at 88th reporting round, and change is detected at 168th round with subject to false alarm probability of 0.01, as shown in the Fig. 4.2. However, for another larger value of mean (0.206), the change point is at 93rd, which is detected at 145th reporting round. The later change was detected soon and the likely reason for this is because of relatively larger mean value. The distribution of generated weight parameters of 10 clients for particular link over the participated reporting rounds are presented in Fig. 4.3.

For the second scenario (to detect change in aggregated parameters), we kept the same value

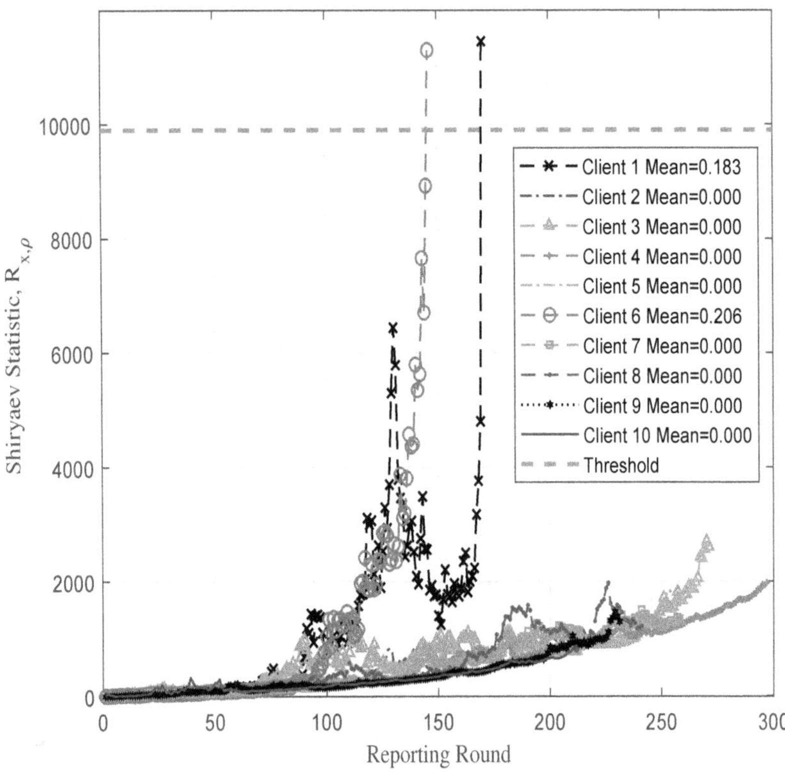

Figure 4.2. Evolution of Shiryaev's algorithm for QCD as per the samples of 10 clients presented in Fig. 4.3.

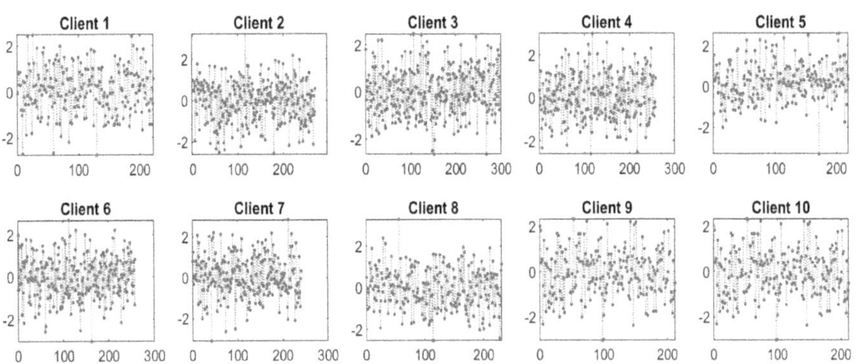

Figure 4.3. Distribution of learning weights (Y-axis values) for 10 clients/participants corresponding to different reporting rounds (X-axis values).

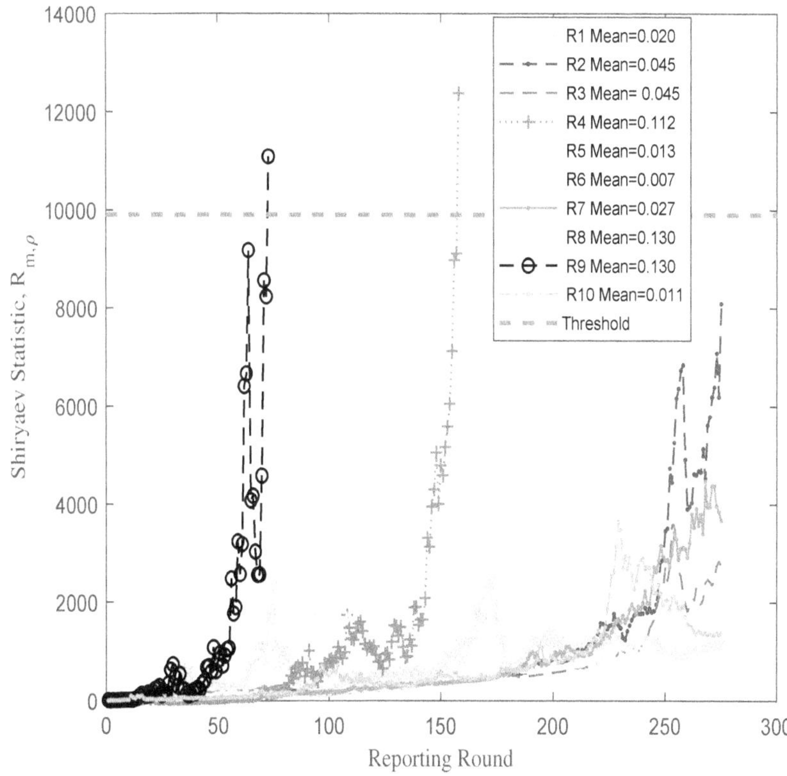

Figure 4.4. Evolution of Shiryaev's algorithm for aggregated parameters of each of the 10 iterations (R1-R10).

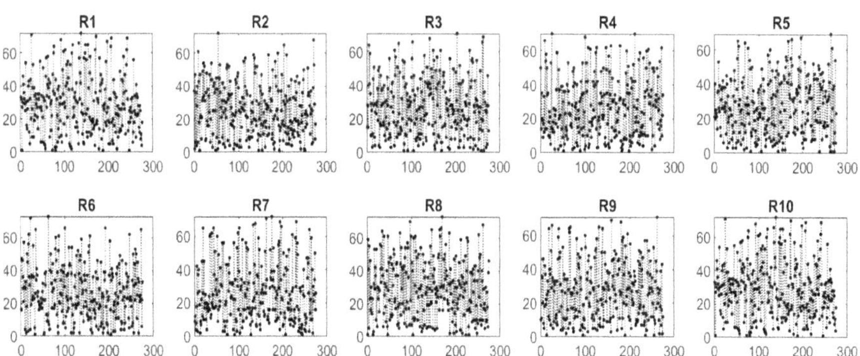

Figure 4.5. Number of malicious clients (Y-axis values) in each reporting round (X-axis values) for 10 iterations (R1-R10).

for the ϱ and A however, we added/changed some FL related parameters. We set the total number of vehicles for one specific learning task as 500. In each reporting round, we selected participants randomly ranging from 20% to 50% of total vehicles. Among these, we randomly set 1 to 30% of the current participants as malicious clients who report perturbed learning parameters (same as first scenario). The number of data points to each participant was assigned a random value from 2000 to 10000. We then applied federated averaging in each reporting round. The number of reporting rounds was assigned a random value from 200 to 300. Finally, we calculated SR statistics $R_{m,\varrho}$ for the values of the aggregated parameters. The experiment was run 10 times and we labeled it as iterations R1-R10 (as shown in Fig. 4.4 and 4.5). The number of reporting rounds for R1-R10 was kept same for simplicity. SR statistics' graph along with the mean of the aggregated parameters' distribution for each iteration are presented in Fig. 4.4 and the number of malicious clients in each reporting round for R1-R10 are shown in Fig. 4.5. As we observed in Fig. 4.4, despite the presence of a number of malicious clients in each reporting round (as shown in Fig. 4.5), there are not much changes in the mean for each run. Seven values of the mean are within 0 to 0.045 and the rest are just greater than 0.1. It is due to multiple reasons. One reason is the random assignment of number of data points to participants and additionally, the federated averaging algorithm is somewhat robust to calculate the expected value. The other reason is the very low perturbation on weight. Most importantly, we wanted to demonstrate that QCD is able to detect even a small change in the distribution of aggregated parameters' value. As shown in the Fig. 4.4, QCD is able to detect change for three mean value (0.130, 0.130 and 0.112).

In summary, in the first scenario (Fig. 4.2), once change is detected, parameters received from anomalous clients can be eliminated from future learning activities to improve the accuracy of the global model. In the second approach (Fig. 4.4), the service provider may choose to earlier better model in case a sufficient change in the model is detected. Finally, it is to be noted that, the proposed approach does not require any extra computation or communication burden on the client-side.

4.6   Chapter Summary

In this chapter, we presented the quickest change detection techniques to detect anomalies in FL for the IoV scenario. We presented two approaches to applying QCD on the server-side. We simulated both the approaches to detect an abnormal change in parameters' values sent by participants as well as to detect an abnormal change in aggregated values. The presented results demonstrated that QCD is able to detect even a small change in the distribution of exchanged parameters Once detected, anomalous clients can be eliminated for future learning activities to improve the accuracy of the model. Moreover, the service provider may choose to earlier better model in case a sufficient change is detected in the model. The proposed approach is efficient since it does not require any extra computation burden or communication burden during transmission for the clients.

CHAPTER 5.   SECURE AND EFFICIENT FEDERATED LEARNING FOR INTERNET OF VEHICLES

5.1   Introduction

IoV has been an active area of research to envision as a solution to achieve an ITS for the past few decades. With the rapid advancement in vehicular technologies, communication technologies, smart sensors, machine learning and others, it is believed that smart autonomous vehicles will solve the existing transportation problems. Major contributors to the transportation problems like congestion and accidents are human errors and ambiguity. IoV, capable of sensing the environment and communicating with neighboring vehicles and infrastructures to exchange every bit of required information for safe navigation, detecting hurdles, optimizing routes and others on-the-fly, offers a true potential to realize ITS for effective traffic management and road safety [4].

In IoV, IEEE 802.11p standard provides dedicated short-range communication (DSRC) based communication, routing protocols and others, to provide the several safety services and the quality services [10]. However, the service providers are constantly seeking to provide varieties of services based on their needs beyond what standard IoV offers. The tremendous volume and vast varieties of data circulated around IoV environment offers a huge potential to apply ML algorithms and create several services and constantly improve the existing services. The services could be anything ranging from safety to quality services with strict to flexible time requirements. The learning problems could be such as optimizing ride-sharing, usage-based insurance policy, driving in new/extreme weather conditions, analyzing driving behaviors, intrusion detection and prevention system (IDS/IPS) and others. The services like driving in new/extreme weather conditions and IDS/IPS are mostly the time sensitive services while others could have time relaxation. Suppose, if an unseen attack emerged in IoV network, IDS/IPS learning model needs to be updated to detect and prevent such attacks as quickly as possible to mitigate any possible disaster. Designing and developing a self-learning and proactive IDS/IPS systems in FL environment has been investigated well in literature (e.g. [103, 104]). These systems have successfully demonstrated to identify unforeseen and unpredictable cyberattacks. In another example, suppose the operating environment of vehicles experienced a sudden extreme weather condition never seen before, then a global model needs to be updated promptly from such vehicles' exchanged parameters to assist them for appropriate navigation or actions.

The common setting of ML where connected devices are required to send their data to a central server and server trains a learning model with the data has raised security, privacy and communication issues. A small delay, privacy, and/or security breach can bring serious consequences in IoV to endanger the life of passengers. In this regard, the FL framework [6] fits better to the IoV application compared to traditional ML approach to work against the flood of data generated in the IoV environment. In FL, ML tasks are performed in the end devices and instead of sending data to the server, only learning model parameters are sent to the central server. Server then aggregates parameters received from the devices and send the global parameters back to the devices. Connected devices then update the learning model with the global parameters. This privacy preserving framework also enhances security by making the life of an attacker difficult to infer from the model parameters. Furthermore, it reduces the communication latency as only the model parameters are exchanged between end devices and server.

Despite so many promising offerings, FL has been questioned against possible poisoning and reverse engineering attacks in recent times [32]. Additionally, a significant rise of heterogeneous smart vehicle sensors and furthermore, communicating over a wireless medium, have extended the attack surface significantly. Wireless communication networks' standards and protocols are more vulnerable than wired communication networks. The mobile and distributed nature of the smart devices exaggerate the security challenges even more. An attacker could easily exploit the vulnerability of the network to lunch different MITM type attacks. Furthermore, a centralized server can bring a single point of failure and trust issues. A server may favor some clients and skew the global model accordingly [105]. A client remains fully unaware of the fairness of the global model. To secure FL, some existing works in literature used techniques like differential privacy [94], secure multi-party computation (SMC) [95], and homomorphic encryption (HE) [96] however, with added computation and communication burden, these techniques could only mitigate man-in-the-middle type attacks but lacks to address single point failure and trust issues associated with a centralized server.

To this end, it looks obvious to accept that a trust-less network system is essential for collaborative learning in IoV. Due to the widespread success of crypto-currencies especially Bitcoin [25] and Ethereum [26], blockchain has been one of the most active areas of research for creating trustless, transparent, and traceable decentralized network for many applications. Automakers likes of BMW, General Motors and others are already on the verge of bringing blockchain to smart vehicles through mobility open blockchain initiative (MOBI) for secure data sharing/trading and various mobility services [106]. Motivated by the true potential of FL to enable to create and enhance varieties IoV services and the strength of BC to create a highly secure network, in this article, we leverage BC on top of FL for IoV to create a trust-less, privacy preserving, audit-able and secure collaborative learning environment.

Over the years, the size and complexity of the machine learning models have been increased significantly so as to achieve better accuracy [107]. Utilizing standard communication and routing protocols, such as the DSRC and Ad-hoc On-demand Distance Vector (AODV) or others could be inefficient to send huge volume of model parameters and perform BC management activities. For example, DSRC is dedicated to broadcast periodic basic safety messages and has limited range and communication speed. In this regard, it would be better for the service provider specific services to utilize cellular technology equipped in the vehicles to carry out all the required ML and BC activities. BC incurs delay due to special BC management activities such as validating, propagating, and recording transactions that nodes in the network are required to perform to make BC trust-less, secure, and audit-able. The delay associated with BC could affect the time sensitive operations of IoV.

We consider the performance of a BC network especially for IoV is equally as important as cyber-security for the IoV and work toward minimizing delay in BC to create an secure and efficient BC empowered FL for IoV. The delay in a BC system depends on the several factors such as complexity of consensus technique, block size, number of nodes, block arrival rate, and others. There are several research efforts to reduce delay in BC such as optimizing block arrival rate [105, 108], using different consensus techniques (e.g. [109, 110]), sharding(e.g. [111, 112], changing block size (e.g. [113]), off-chain transactions (e.g. [114, 115], different approaches for peer selection (e.g. [116, 117]. However, a single solution could not be sufficient to address the system delay present in blockchain instead, these approaches complement each other to make blockchain system scalable.

Information dissemination delay in a BC is the time taken to disseminate a transaction/block through out the network. It encapsulates blockchain management activities consisting of validating, forwarding, and recording transaction/block. Whenever a transaction is generated or a block is created, the delay can be minimized if a BC system could disseminate such information throughout the network faster. Moreover, when the information dissemination delay increases, it correspondingly increases the probability of forking[1] and which opens the opportunities for attackers to lunch attacks such as double spending attack and withholding attack [118]. In this work, we primarily focus on the peer selection approach considering that an appropriate peer selection strategy has the potential to disseminate information faster and reduce the system delay considerably.

Considering the IoV network where vehicles take part as the nodes of a blockchain network is highly dynamic in nature. The network topology in IoV changes so frequently compared to other applications where network nodes remain mostly static and available most of the time. In IoV, the availability of peers is likely to depend on several factors including the time period of the current journey, geographical time, and location. Delay of the network can be minimized if we could spread the information faster; however, the unavailability of peers affects the information dissemination. Taking this into account, we work toward making blockchain based IoV efficient by applying an appropriate peer selection strategy.

---

[1]Forking is a situation in the blockchain network when network has inconsistent records of transactions.

In literature, blockchain has been mostly studied taking bitcoin as a reference as it is the first and the most popular blockchain network and has gained explosive growth in terms of total users, transactions and value in recent years [116]. For this paper, we also make our assumptions in reference to bitcoin. The performance modeling and analysis of blockchain network have been studied mostly using the Random Graph (RG) network model (e.g. [119]. Bitcoin by default is a RG where nodes choose peers randomly [118]. However, there are few approaches that select peers based on Regular Lattice (RL) network topology (e.g. [120]) and small world (SW) network topology (e.g. [116]. A SW network which exhibits the characteristics of both the RL and RG is highly clustered like RL network, yet has small characteristic path lengths like RG which makes it highly effective in regional specialization with efficient information transfer [121, 122].

In [116], Park et al. considered geographical positions of the bitcoin nodes and experimented with selecting 8 peers in different combinations to study the information dissemination in the bitcoin network. The combination is chosen such that it also resembles RL, RG and SW networks. Authors demonstrated that selecting the peers in almost equal proportion from near, mid and far geographical regions (3-3-2) was able to spread the information faster compared to other selection approaches. For our work, we use the same SW peer selection strategy as proposed in [116] however, we also incorporate vehicles' count in each region and other additional informed decisions which are specific to IoV network. In IoV, a vehicle may leave the network after finishing the current journey. In some geographical locations, vehicles may not be available due to different time zone. We consider all these information into account to design a better peer selection strategy which could have the potential to accelerate message propagation.

This article uses simulation based approach to design an IoV network and observe the information dissemination delay performances. A graph based approach is used to represent the IoV network and analyze the delay and compare the performance of the proposed approach in the scenarios where we don't use informed decision vs. when we use informed decisions. To the best of our knowledge, this work is novel and unique to address the propagation delay of blockchain by accelerating information spreading for IoV application. On top of it, we also incorporate informed decisions which are specific to IoV.

Specifically, our contributions include:

1. Investigate message dissemination delay for blockchain enabled IoV network under small world network based peer selection strategy.

2. Investigate delay under dynamic network topology of IoV using graph based approach.

3. Investigate the delay performance of the blockchain for IoV incorporating informed decisions specific to IoV.

The primary motivation behind our work is to enhance the privacy and security of FL for IoV by leveraging blockchain. However, we strongly consider that the IoV operations are delay sensitive and so, the blockchain for IoV needs to be efficient. Taking this into account, we investigate to minimize the delay of blockchain network from different perspective that can be easily integrated with other existing approaches to further reducing the system delay of blockchain network.

The rest of the paper is organized as follows. Section 5.2 discusses related works. Section 5.3 presents the system model and discusses the working mechanism of the proposed BC based FL for IoV. The proposed peer selection strategy and the information dissemination delay formulation are presented in Section 5.4. Section 5.5 presents simulation results and discusses performance of our proposed approach. Finally, Section 5.6 concludes the paper.

5.2 Related Work

Blockchain for IoV has already been well investigated for several applications like data management and protection (e.g. [123]), forensic application (e.g. [124]), traffic control and management (e.g. [125]), data trading (e.g. [126],content broadcasting (e.g. [127]) and others. However, these works do not investigate the scalability of BC that may hinder the performance of IoV.

Some recent works have considered reputation scheme for assessing the credibility of vehicular nodes that takes part in blokchain network for IoV (e.g. [128–130]) for enhancing security and performance of Blockchain and IoV. Kudva et al. [131] proposed new trust based consensus technique named as Proof of Driving (PoD) to create efficient and scalable blockchain for Vehicular-Ad-Hoc-Network (VANET). This technique randomly select honest miners for generating blocks efficiently. This trust based approach used a filtering technique to detect and eliminate malicious miners in the VANET. However, these works primarily focused on reputation/trust scheme in blockchain network whose purpose is to create a trustless, secure and robust network taking fully account of presence of malicious nodes in the network. These works mainly focuses on blockchain component and do not investigate network topology.

BAFFLE [132] replaced central server and proposed to use smart contract for aggregation. Shiva et al. [105] performed comprehensive analysis for deriving optimal block arrival rate in blockchain based federated learning for IoV considering network system dynamics for the end-to-end system delay. Although, this work explores several aspects of IoV but lacks to address the change in network topology due to the mobility of vehicles/peers.

Zhang et al. [110] work towards optimizing the throughput and the quality of services of blockchain based IoV considering blocksize of blockchain nodes, the number of consensus nodes, reliable features of each vehicle, and the number of producing blocks for each block producer in a joint optimization problem. In the this approach requires a trust quantification for vehicles and furthermore, it used redundant Byzantine fault tolerance (RBFT) consensus rule where consensus operations are delegated to some trusted primary nodes. Its performance degrades when primary nodes become malicious and moreover, it is not robust and secure as compared to the Proof-of-Work consensus algorithm.

In a survey of blockchain for the IoV towards ITS [133], none of the surveyed works investigated information spreading delay which is one of the main contributors to reducing the system delay of the blockchain network. Similarly, in another survey on blockchain applications to improve the operation and security of transportation systems [134], the surveyed works also lack to address the delay which is quite important from the security aspect too.

In literature, several works have modeled and analyzed propagation delay using a graph approach and devising peer selection strategy(e.g. [116, 117, 119, 135, 136]) however, these are better apply to the network where topology mostly remains static and may not perform as desired for IoV where network topology changes frequently and availability of peers are likely to be determined by the current journey and location of vehicles. To the best of our knowledge, this is the first work to investigate propagation delay using the peer selection strategy for IoV which has special characteristics due to mobility.

5.3 Blockchain Enabled Federated Learning for Internet of Vehicles

In this section, we first present the proposed system model and then discuss the working mechanism of the proposed BC based FL for IoV.

5.3.1 System Model

The proposed system model (Fig. 5.1) for SEB-FLV consists of heterogeneous vehicles equipped with various smart sensors, dedicated short-range communication (DSRC) technology (such as the IEEE 802.11p standard devices) and faster cellular communication like 5G. Vehicles communicate to each other and road side units (RSU) to share and exchange Iov standard basic safety messages, up-to-date traffic information, active navigation, and other roadside services using DSRC based communication. Each vehicle takes part in the network as a blockchain node and plays a role of miner too while performing BC based FL operations. Also, each vehicle contains a ML model to perform ML tasks locally and necessary BC components (e.g. digital ledger) and software to perform BC related activities. The digital ledger contains all the chronological history of blocks containing the local updates received from clients and the global updates generated from those local updates. All the blockchain and FL operations are performed using cellular communication. The wireless communication (depicted by yellow link) is meant to represent both DSRC based communication to exchange IoV standard messages and cellular communication to exchange FL and BC related messages.

Installing sufficient roadside infrastructure requires high investment which limits the dependency on RSU for BC operations otherwise, BC network may experience significant delay to make the network vulnerable to attacks. With this assumption, the proposed system model consists of a blockchain network of vehicles only where vehicles transmit/forward local updates/block to the network using peer based message forwarding approach. For illustration only, the system model (Fig. 5.1) shows peer information for one vehicle (depicted as blue arrow)); however, in the network, every node has a number of peers based on the peer selection protocol of blockchain. The default approach to select peers in a BC system is random however, the figure aims to depict selection of peers following proposed SW approach where peers are selected from near, mid and far geographical locations. In blockchain enabled IoV, RSU with high speed link can be employed as the relay gateway for faster message propagation however, considering a homogeneous network of vehicles only enables better delay estimation.

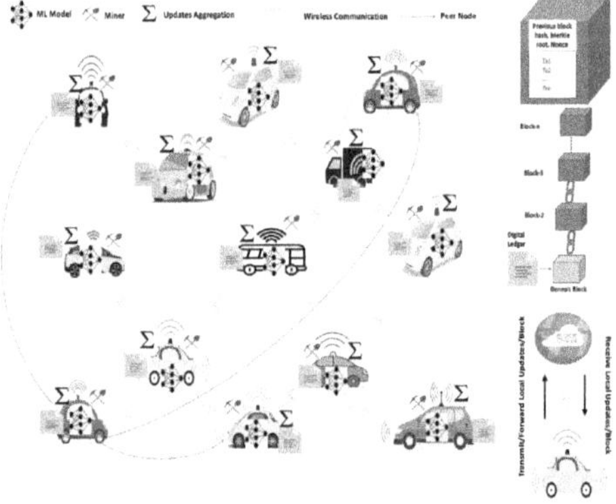

Figure 5.1. System Model of Blockchain Enabled FL for IoV

The larger the blockchain network grows, the more secure the network becomes [137]. Most importantly, the higher the number of miners, the harder it is for attackers to take control of the network. Also, increasing the number of miners increases the probability of solving the cryptographic consensus puzzle faster which enhances the block arrival rate. For all the terminologies related to blockchain and its working principle, we encourage readers to refer to articles e.g. [25, 138]. Smart cars are likely to be equipped with high computational power and storage capacity, so in the proposed approach, all vehicles in the network act as miners and participate in a block creation process. However, an increase in network size is also likely to increase system delay due to increased traffic, propagation and verification tasks. To address this, we propose SW network based peer selection incorporating informed decisions to spread the message faster in the network.

5.3.2 Blockchain for Federated Learning for Internet of Vehicles

BC is a decentralized distributed network that uses public key cryptography, distributed digital ledger, and consensus algorithms as core components for creating secure, transparent and auditable network to allow people/devices to communicate in a trust-less manner without the presence of any intermediaries. In the proposed BC enabled FL for IoV, when a set of vehicles are selected in a communication round, these vehicles perform local ML tasks and transmit their local updates to the BC network as a blockchain transaction. The updates from the vehicles are verified by the network nodes. A set of powerful computing nodes termed miners collect such updates, aggregate them and put all these in a data structure which is called a block. It is likely that due to several reasons, all the selected vehicles may not report in the current round. To overcome this scenario, miners wait until either a time out is reached or all the devices report their updates (although it is quite unlikely), whichever satisfies early. With the collected updates, miners compete to create a valid address for the new block. A successful miner transmits the newly created valid block to the network and the network nodes validate the block and update its local ledger by chaining the new block cryptographically on top of the last created block. Moreover, the chain of blocks also maintains the chronological order for all the valid blocks starting from the first block called as a genesis block. The fairness of updation of the global model parameters is validated by all the nodes from the local updates used for aggregation.

In each communication round, a subset of vehicles are invited through an invitation message created with consensus among miners. A invitation message contains id of invitee and communication round number and these can serve as a mechanism to ensure only the invited vehicle participates only in the invited communication round. IoV may experience communication issue due to noise, interference, channel congestion, and others which may cause local updates from previous rounds still floating around the network. So, the invitation message can serve as a basis that only the local updates belonging to the current communication round are considered while creating a block and the rest are discarded from the network.

One of the prime advantages BC offers is that data is always readily available to each network participant. With this property, each vehicle once selected in a communication round can locally access the most recent global updates and train its local model. This is advantageous to overcome the delay that exists in the conventional FL framework where a centralized server needs to create a global model first and then distribute it to the clients. Furthermore, this blockchain based approach eliminates the single server's trust and failure issues too.

5.4 Peer Selection Strategy and Information Dissemination Delay Estimation: Proposed Approach

When a vehicle receives or generates a transaction or a block of transactions (tx/bk), it uses a push-based approach to forward the information. Instead of flooding the network with redundant copies, when a node receives a tx/bk, it first sends an inventory message (*inv*) to its peers. An *inv* contains the hash of the message which assists a peer to identify whether it already has the tx/bk or not. If a peer does not have it yet, it issues a *getdata* message which contains the hash of the requested message. Upon receiving *getdata*, a node sends the tx/bk to the requester. Whenever a tx/bk is generated at any of the nodes in the network, each node follows this protocol to spread it though-out the network.

5.4.1 Peer Selection Strategy

In a blockchain network, by construction, the nodes form a random graph where nodes join and leave the network randomly [118]. When a node joins the network, it requires to connect to other blockchain nodes called peers to be able to propagate each tx/bk. The information about active nodes that a node may select as peers is gathered through peer discovery process. Once active nodes are discovered, the node may choose the peers to connect to from the available list. The default behavior of bitcoin software to choose its peers is random and the software defines up to the maximum of 8 outgoing connections and 117 incoming connections [139].

Information can be spread to a network using three network approaches which are regular lattice, random graph and small world network. In RL topology, each node selects its peers which are in closest proximity. Due to this, it has high clustering coefficients but lacks global connection. A lack of global connection increases the average path length of the network when the network grows wider. In random topology, as all peers are chosen randomly, it is likely to form high global connections but lacks clustering. By which, it exhibits the properties of low clustering coefficient and low average path length. A SW network however, is formed by rewiring the links of the lattice network randomly with some probability p [140]. From the RL network, SW and RG networks can be formed by varying p. If $p = 0$, the network is regarded as a lattice network, and when $p = 1$, that means all edges are rewired randomly and it builds RG. For other values of p, the network is called SW network. A SW network holds both long range connections with remote nodes as well as short range connections with neighboring nodes. So, it exhibits the useful properties (high clustering coefficient and low average path length) of both LN and RN that are likely to result in faster information spreading.

Like joining, a node may leave the network randomly and its address could linger for several hours in the network before other nodes remove it from their known addresses set [118]. The probability of nodes' leaving the network in IoV is higher due to several reasons. This could change the connectivity of the network and affect the message dissemination latency if a proper peer selection strategy is not employed. In bitcoin, the default number of peers (outgoing connections) for a node is 8 however, in practice the average number of connections is 32 [118].

Let us assume each vehicle selects the same number of peers denoted as T_p. Using GPS locations of vehicles, for each vehicle, we consider the farthest distance to any vehicle and divide it into 3 equal parts to identify geographical regions as near, mid, and far. Exploiting the properties of the SW network to disseminate information faster, each node then selects its peers from each region. For V as the set of vehicles, the proportion of the total number of peers for each vehicle to the total number vehicles can be represented as $\frac{T_p}{|V|}$. Let, $|V_n|, |V_m|,$ and $|V_f|$ represent the total number of vehicles in near, mid, and far regions respectively. Each vehicle then selects its peers from each region in proportion to the number of vehicles in the region as,

$$T_{p,n} = \lceil \frac{T_p}{|V|}|V_n| \rceil$$

$$T_{p,m} = \lceil \frac{T_p}{|V|}|V_m| \rceil \tag{5.1}$$

$$T_{p,f} = T_p - T_{p,n} - T_{p,m}$$

Where, $T_{p,n}$, $T_{p,m}$, and $T_{p,f}$ are the number of peers from near, mid, and far regions respectively. For each node, peers from the near region are selected based on closest geographical proximity while those are selected randomly for mid and far regions. The harvesine formula [141] for great circle distance is considered to calculate the distance between any two vehicles. For latitudes as ϕ_i and ϕ_j and longitudes as λ_i and λ_j for two vehicles i and j in radian respectively, the harvesine distance between them in meters can be expressed as,

$$d_{ij} = 2R\sin^{-1}\sqrt{sin^2(\frac{\phi_i - \phi_j}{2} + cos(\phi_i)cos(\phi_j)sin^2(\frac{\lambda_i - \lambda_j}{2})} \tag{5.2}$$

Where R is the radius of the earth whose value is 6371×10^3 meters.

After peer selection, the SW network is modeled as a graph and information dissemination latency is estimated through graph analysis.

5.4.2 Information Dissemination Delay Estimation

Let, $G = (V, E)$ represents the blockchain network of vehicles where G is a directed graph for the set of vehicles participating as blockchain nodes V and the set of edges E between network nodes. Each edge $e_{ij} \in E$ represents an outgoing connection from node i to node j. So, e_{ij} in fact represents only the forward relation that a node j is the peer of another node i but not the opposite. For the set of vehicles V, the set of edges E in graph G can be expressed as adjacency matrix A of

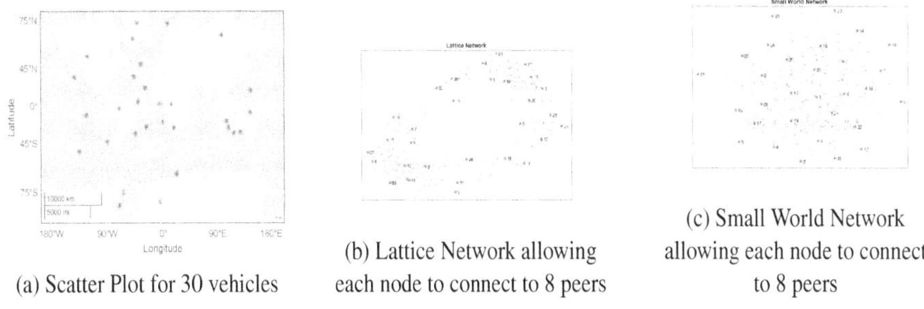

(a) Scatter Plot for 30 vehicles   (b) Lattice Network allowing each node to connect to 8 peers   (c) Small World Network allowing each node to connect to 8 peers

Figure 5.2. Examples for RL and SW graphs corresponding to Fig. 5.2a

size $|V| \times |V|$ where for each element $a_{ij} \in A$ can be expressed as,

$$
a_{ij} = \begin{cases} 1 & \text{if } e_{ij} \in E \\ 0 & \text{if } e_{ij} \notin E \end{cases} \tag{5.3}
$$

When a node generates a tx/bk, it follows propagation protocol to forward the message to its peers. Peers also use the same protocol to forward the message to their peers and eventually spread the information throughout the network. In the SW network, a peer could be at any hop link distance as per the size of the network. It is not feasible to know the actual topology of the IoV network that could be used to find the number of links to reach a peer and estimate the delay. For best-effort approximation, we use the assigned location information of vehicles and form a RL network to approximate the number of hops to reach any peer for the SW network. To form a RL network in a similar setting, each node selects all of its peers (T_p) from its closest geographical proximity. In a RL network, for any node, it is assumed that all its peers are in one hop link distance. For simplicity, we assume that each one hop connection between vehicles has the same communication link speed.

To illustrate peer selection as an example, we assigned a random GPS coordinates to 30 vehicles as shown in Figure 5.2a and form the RL and SW graphs accordingly allowing each node to connect to $T_p = 8$ peers as shown in Figures 5.2b and 5.2c respectively.

Let, A_L and A_S denote the adjacency matrices for the RL and SW networks respectively. In

101

A_L, if the entry for $a_{ij}^L = 1$ where $a_{ij}^L \in A_L$, peer j of node i is at one hop link distance. With this assumption, for each node, the adjacency matrix A_L also lists all the nodes which are in one hop link distance. With A_L, we generate shortest path matrix S_L of size $|V| \times |V|$ for all the nodes where each value $s_{ij}^L \in S_L$ gives the shortest distance for any node i to reach any other node j in terms of the number of edges. With this information, we approximate how many hops link distance j is away from i. However, adjacency matrix of A_S should be interpreted differently where $a_{ij}^S = 1$ ($a_{ij}^S \in A_S$) only represents j as the peer of i. As mentioned earlier, j could be at any hops link distance as per the size of the network.

To estimate the delay to spread a message in RL is straightforward compared to the SW network. When a node generates a tx/bk, it follows propagation protocol to forward the message to its peers at one hop distance. Similarly, peers use the same strategy to forward the received message to their peers (which are also at one hop distance) and eventually spread the information throughout the network. Following the propagation protocol, peer nodes are required to process the *inv* and *getdata* messages. Furthermore, whenever a node receives a tx/bk, it performs validation to confirm the integrity of the message. Now, we devise the message dissemination delay for each node in the SW network when a message is first generated at that node. For comparison and better understandability only, we first formulate the delay for the RL network and then extend it to formulate the delay for the SW network. For simplicity, we do not consider noise and interference, channel congestion, and others that may present in the IoV environment and which could affect the delay.

Let, $\mathcal{M}$ is a message (tx/bk) generated at node i and $\mathcal{D}_{ij}^L$ is the propagation delay for node i to deliver $\mathcal{M}$ to all other nodes j in RL network, where $i = 1$ to $|V|$, $j = 1$ to $|V|$ and $j \neq i$. Here, $\mathcal{D}_{ij} = 0$ for $i = j$.

For T_i, T_g, T_m are the time taken to transmit *inv*, *getdata* and message $\mathcal{M}$ to one hop distant node and P_i, P_g, P_m are the processing delays at each node to process *inv*, *getdata* and message $\mathcal{M}$

respectively then $\mathcal{D}_{ij}^L$ can be expressed as,

$$\mathcal{D}_{ij}^L = s_{ij}^L(T_i + P_i + T_g + P_g + T_m + P_m) \tag{5.4}$$

In RL network, to transmit $\mathcal{M}$ originated at node i to node j, node i first sends *inv* to its peer (say i_1) at one hop link distance. Node i_1 in response, sends *getdata* to i and finally, node i transmit $\mathcal{M}$ to i_1. Node i_1 follows same process to transmit $\mathcal{M}$ to its peer (say i_2) and the process is repeated until $\mathcal{M}$ is delivered to node j. s_{ij}^L in equation (5.4) gives the number of links to reach from node i to node j as mentioned earlier.

Now, we devise message dissemination delay $\mathcal{D}_{ij}^S$ for SW network. Let, S_S is the shortest path matrix generated from A_S.

When j is peer of i, $\mathcal{D}_{ij}^S$ can be expressed as,

$$D_{ij}^S = (s_{ij}^L - 1)(T_i + T_g + T_m) + (T_i + P_i + T_g + P_g + T_m + P_m) \tag{5.5}$$

Otherwise,

$$\begin{aligned}
D_{ij}^S = &((s_{ii_1}^L - 1)(T_i + T_g + T_m)+ \\
&(T_i + P_i + T_g + P_g + T_m + P_m))+ \\
&((s_{i_1 i_2}^L - 1)(T_i + T_g + T_m)+ \\
&(T_i + P_i + T_g + P_g + T_m + P_m)) + ... \\
&((s_{i_{n-1}j}^L - 1)(T_i + T_g + T_m)+ \\
&(T_i + P_i + T_g + P_g + T_m + P_m))
\end{aligned} \tag{5.6}$$

In equation (5.5), all intermediate nodes (which are non-peers) between i to j only forward *inv*, *getdata* and $\mathcal{M}$ and do not perform processing. Only the peer node j process these messages as reflected in the equation. s_{xy}^L provides the actual number of hops to reach from node any x to node any node y.

In equation (5.6), $i_1, i_2, ...i_{n-1}$ are the sequence of nodes in the shortest path of S_S to reach from i to j. So, in the sequence $i_1, i_2, ...i_{n-1}$, i_1 is the immediate peer of node i where as other nodes in the sequence are the peer of preceding node. Similarly, all non-peer nodes exist between i to j only forward *inv*, *getdata* and message $\mathcal{M}$ do not perform processing.

For $|V|$ vehicles, we assign initial GPS locations along with the destination locations. To incorporate the mobility factor, we consider destination distance for each vehicle and observe the change in network topology every X kilo meters (km) for $i = 1$ to I number of intervals. Assuming the same speed for every vehicle, if the cumulative travelled distance iX is greater than the destination distance of a vehicle, the vehicle has already finished its journey and could leave the network. Vehicles' availability is also likely to be influenced by the time zone of its geographical location. For example, the traffic during day is mostly higher than the night time. At day time, the possibility of starting a new journey after finishing current journey is higher compared to night time.

To incorporate this, an unavailability probability ϱ is assigned to each vehicle whose value is higher for vehicles which are in night time zone and lower if they are in day time zone. Based on probability ϱ, if a vehicle is not available again, it is removed from the network otherwise, a new destination coordinate is assigned. We identify time zone using longitude of vehicles and taking 2:00 PM at coordinated universal time (UTC) as a reference. With mentioned assumptions, at each travelled distance iX km, we remove unavailable vehicles and update SW matrix accordingly. On course of journey, initial RL may not still hold the property of RL network due to the change in network topology because of mobility. However, the delay for SW at any instant is found based on a true RL (choosing vehicles in closest proximity as peers) as per the current topology. So, at each interval i, we create RL network according to the current topology and estimate delay for SW accordingly. Let, $|V_i|$ be the number of vehicles available at interval i then, proportion of vehicles unavailable at that moment is $U_i = \frac{(|V|-|V_i|)}{|V|}$. Using U_i, number of peers for RL is updated as $round(U_i * T_p)$.

While moving to destination, we find the current GPS coordinates for available vehicles at every travelled distance iX using source and destination coordinates. First, we find the bearing and then use source GPS coordinate and travelled distance iX to find current coordinate referring [142].

For latitudes as ϕ_s and ϕ_d and longitudes as λ_s and λ_d for source and destination GPS of a vehicle in radian respectively, bearing in radian can be expressed as,

$$\theta = (sin(\lambda_d - \lambda_s)cos(\phi_d),$$
$$cos(\phi_s)sin(\phi_d) - sin(\phi_s)cos(\phi_d)cos(\lambda_d - \lambda_s)) \tag{5.7}$$

For intervals $i = 1$ to I, latitude and longitude ϕ_i and λ_i respectively can be expressed as,

$$\phi_i = sin^{-1}(sin(\phi_s)cos(\delta) + cos(\phi_s)sin(\delta)cos(\theta)$$
$$\lambda_i = \lambda_s + (sin(\theta)sin(\delta)cos(\phi_s),$$
$$cos(\delta) - sin(\phi_s)sin(\phi_i)) \tag{5.8}$$

Where, $\delta = \frac{iX}{R}$ is the angular distance and R is the earth's radius.

The unavailability of vehicles which could be the peers of some vehicles is likely to increase the message dissemination delay for those vehicles. To overcome this, we propose to use informed decision in which each vehicle is assigned peers based on the availability information. In this approach, for each vehicle $v_i \in V$, v_i selects T_p, n peers from near region using the same approach as mentioned in Equation 5.1. However, in case of mid and far regions, if distance to travel for randomly selected vehicle $v_j \in V$, $v_i \neq v_j \geq$ to distance to travel for v_i, v_j is selected as a peer (only if the incoming connections to v_i is not saturated) otherwise, v_j is selected based on some probability α if v_j belongs to day time region and with probability β if v_j belongs to night time region where $\alpha > \beta$. The main aim behind this approach is to make peers available during the journey.

In the next section, we simulate our proposed approach to estimate the message dissemination delay under both uninformed and informed decision scenarios and present the performance evaluation.

5.5 Performance Evaluation

This section presents the evaluation approach and simulation results for the proposed approach discussed in Section 5.4.

5.5.1 Evaluation Approach

We implemented our proposed approach using Matlab as a simulation tool. Random GPS coordinates were assigned to each of the $|V|$ vehicles where the values of latitudes range from -170 to 170 degree and longitudes range from -80 to 80 degree. For each vehicle, the distances to all other vehicles were calculated using Equation 5.2 and stored in ascending order. Taking the total number of peers as $T_p = 8$ (default number of the peers in bitcoin), RL and SW networks were formed according to the approach discussed in Section 5.4. All these networks were then represented by adjacency matrices and for each matrix, we created the shortest path matrix.

In a real scenario, the one-hop neighboring vehicles are at varying distances likely to have different communication latencies. However, for simplicity, we assume the same the communication latency for all one-hop links. Similarly, all the one hop links speed is assumed as 100 Megabits-per-second (Mbps). Additionally, other assumptions we made are the same processing capability and the same processing delay for each vehicle. Tx/bk size in a blockchain based FL depends on the size of a ML model used. Furthermore, the size of a block also depends on the number of nodes that participated in a communication round and it could vary from round to round. For the simulation, we considered the propagation delay for the block only and the delay is estimated assuming a block is generated at each node and is required to disseminate at every other node. For simplicity, we assign the same block size for all communication rounds as 1 Megabyte (MB), which is the maximum block size in bitcoin. Considering the size of recent ML models, this could be a small estimate however, the main purpose here is to compare the performance of the peer selection strategy for uninformed and informed decision scenarios under the same parameter setting. For the rest of the paper, we term the uniformed scenario as scenario I and the informed scenario as scenario II. The processing time for *inv*, *getdata* and tx/bk depends on the computational power of nodes and the size of these messages. For simplicity, the block processing time was assigned as 150*ms* by taking the reference of estimation for the 1 MB block size provided in [143]. The size of *inv* and *getdata* in bitcoin has a small constant size of 61 Bytes in most cases [118]. The processing time for *inv* and *getdata* were assigned as 1*ms* which is significantly low compared to block processing time. It is due to the fact that the block processing involves validating all the transactions which requires access to the disc.

To simulate the mobility, each vehicle is assigned destination's latitude randomly between the extreme range of latitude from vehicle's position that is $(-90 - \phi_i, 90 - \phi_i)$ and the same for longitude as $(-180 - \phi_i, 180 - \phi_i)$. At every $X = 16$ km for the number of intervals $I = 4$, we updated graphs and measured the delay according to the current network topology.

On course of travel, we observed some nodes were unreachable due to the unavailability of vehicles selecting them as peers resulting in infinite propagation delay. Such values were discarded and the delays were calculated from the rest. We assigned unavailability probability $\varrho = 0.90$ and 0.60 for vehicles in night time zone and day time zone respectively. The values for α and β were assigned as 0.3 and 0.1 respectively. For all the mentioned parameter settings, the simulation was carried out for varying number of vehicles as $|V| = 200, 300, 500$ and 1000. The simulation was repeated 5 times to take the average of the performance metrics. The results of the simulation observed at each travel interval are presented next.

5.5.2 Results

The performances of proposed approach were measured in terms of the percentage of vehicles unavailable, average SW network path length, maximum propagation delay and average propagation delay. The results were observed at each travel interval for varying number of vehicles as shown in Figures 5.3, 5.4, 5.5 and 5.6.

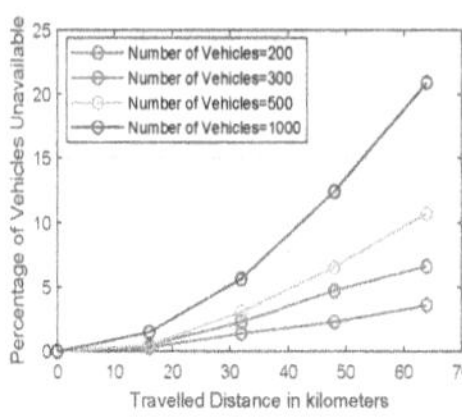

Figure 5.3. Percentage of unavailable vehicles at each travelled distance interval

In reference to 2:00 p.m. UTC time, 8:00 a.m. to 8:0 p.m. was taken as the day time while the rest was considered as the night time. At each travel interval, a random destinations to the vehicles which finished its journey were reassigned based on their time zone information and unavailability probability ϱ. Figure 5.3 shows the percentage of the total vehicles which were unavailable at each travel interval.

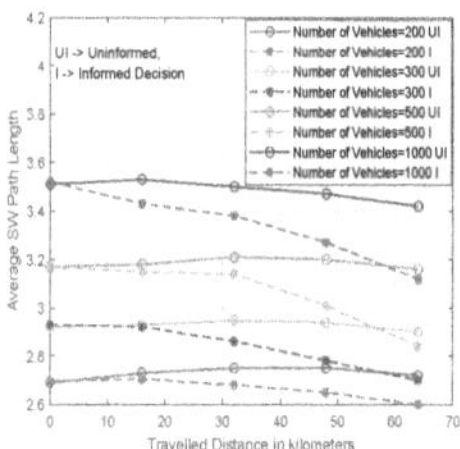

Figure 5.4. Average SW path length at each travelled distance interval

Figure 5.4 shows the comparison of average value of the SW path length to reach any of the nodes between scenario I and scenario II measured at each travel interval for $|V| = 200, 300, 500$ and 1000. As shown in the figure, on course of travel, the average path length for scenario II is considerably lower compared to scenario I. The reason for this trend is, in scenario II, nodes are likely to select peers which have higher availability during the travel. That also means nodes with lower availability are less likely to be selected as peers so as to receive messages and forward to other nodes. When such nodes are removed from network, the network becomes smaller resulting in lower path length. However, in scenario I, as peers were selected randomly, the peers with lower travel distance when became unavailable, broke the existing shortest paths to reach other nodes. Because of this, the average SW path in scenario I did not decrease as much as scenario II despite the network becoming smaller due to removal of unavailable vehicles.

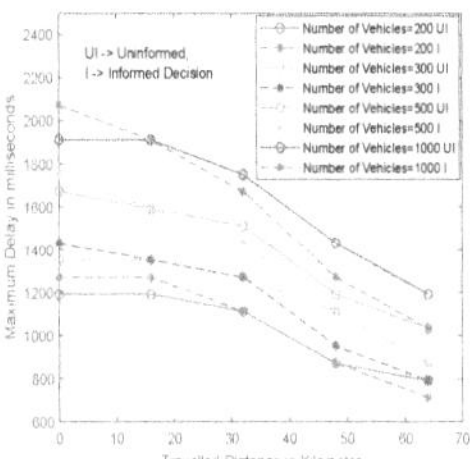

Figure 5.5. Maximum information dissemination delay at each travelled distance interval

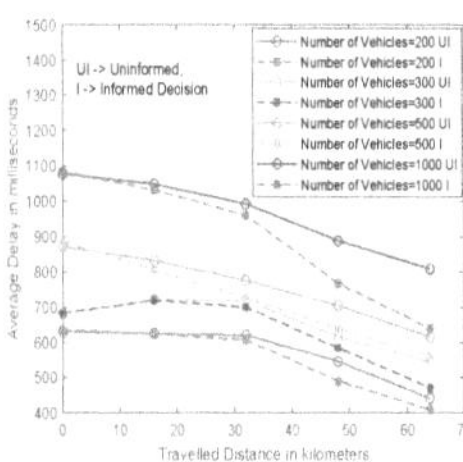

Figure 5.6. Average information dissemination delay at each travelled distance interval

As shown in Figure 5.5, the maximum information dissemination delay for any node for scenario I and scenario II follows the similar decreasing trend for all $|V|$. Initially, the maximum delay observed is significantly higher in both the scenarios but, it keeps on decreasing (subject to removing unreachable nodes) as network becomes smaller with the removal of unavailable vehicles from the network. The decreasing rate however, is higher for scenario II. In scenario II, the chances to select vehicles which are likely to be unavailable as peers are low. When such vehicles are removed from the network, it does not affect the shortest path to reach any other nodes.

The average delay observed as shown in figure 5.6 follows similar trend due to similar reason but it is significantly lower than the maximum delay observed. Due to the very low indegree of some of the nodes resulted to the higher value of maximum delay. Although the average SW path changes slightly in scenario I, the delay was still reduced as it is calculated based on the number of hops to reach any nodes based on the current topology of RL network.

Although the information dissemination delays observed are of higher values, they are estimated considering BC network of vehicles only. The inclusion of road side infrastructures as a relay network could reduce delay significantly. The primary purpose of this study is to suggest a better peer selection strategy appropriate to the IoV network.

5.6 Chapter Summary

In this chapter, we proposed blockchain based federated learning to enable a secure collaborative learning environment for internet of vehicles. A small world network based peer selection strategy was employed for efficient information dissemination in the network. Informed decisions were incorporated in the peer selection strategy to enhance faster information propagation. We used graph based approach to represent the BC network of vehicles and analyse the propagation delay. The simulation results showed that the inclusion of informed decision is highly effective to reduce the information dissemination delay and make BC based IoV efficient.

CHAPTER 6. CONCLUSION

An ITS is on the verge of becoming reality in the near future. Despite the promising potentials an ITS can offer, it possesses several performance and security challenges. Taking these into account, this dissertation proposed to design and develop a fully secure and efficient IoV for ITS.

To address the aforementioned challenges, this dissertation first presented a novel clustering approach to mitigate the broadcast storm problem which could arise due to the high vehicular density. The clustering approach considered important behavioral parameters and a current journey parameter which were then used to calculate a CFS for each vehicle. In a region, a vehicle with the highest CFS is elected as a CH which then manages communication inside and outside of the cluster. The selection of CH, the cluster management activities and the CH's roles were designed in such a way that it was able to improve the cluster stability as well as the the network performance of IoV. The improved performances were demonstrated through numerical results by comparing with existing approaches.

The vast amount of data captured by distributed smart vehicles equipped with various sensors presents an excellent opportunity to utilize ML techniques to enhance intelligent transportation systems. However, the growing number of smart vehicles could pose a communication challenge to implementing machine learning centrally in the IoV. To address this issue, this dissertation next proposed a novel approach that applies the Mahalanobis distance metric to the data sent by vehicles to sample valuable observations before sending it to a server via Road Side Infrastructure (RSI). The sampling ratio is adjusted according to the current network condition. The sampled observations are collected centrally, and ML tasks are performed to produce intelligent services. The effectiveness of the proposed approach was verified by comparing it with an unsampled scenario.

Considering the presence of malicious clients in FL for IoV environment, this dissertation took the next step to present a novel approach to apply QCD to analyze model parameters in FL and detect such clients. The proposed approach applied Shiryaev's QCD techniques in server side in two scenarios. In one scenario, QCD analyzes the history of model parameters sent by each client and detect anomaly. In other scenario, QCD analyzes the history of aggregated model parameters to detect any anomaly in the global model. The performances of both scenarios were presented through numerical results.

Considering the possible MITM type attacks, single point of failure and trust issues in FL, this dissertation finally proposed to design an efficient BC based FL for IoV. This study primarily focused on making BC based system efficient by investigating the information dissemination delay in BC. In this regard, this work proposed a novel approach to use a SW network based peer selection strategy for BC based IoV network. Furthermore, this work also incorporated additional informed decision that are specific to IoV scenario in the peer selection strategy. The performance demonstrated that the inclusion of informed decision resulted to even better information spreading to reduce information dissemination delay.